Diabetic Meal Prep Cookbook #2020

Affordable, Easy & Delicious Diabetic Diet Recipes to Lower Blood Sugar & Reverse Diabetes | 30-Day Meal Plan to Kickstart Your Healthy Lifestyle

Barbon Jamsen

© Copyright 2020 Barbon Jamsen - All Rights Reserved.

In no way is it legal to reproduce, duplicate, or transmit any part of this document by either electronic means or in printed format. Recording of this publication is strictly prohibited, and any storage of this material is not allowed unless with written permission from the publisher. All rights reserved.

The information provided herein is stated to be truthful and consistent, in that any liability, regarding inattention or otherwise, by any usage or abuse of any policies, processes, or directions contained within is the solitary and complete responsibility of the recipient reader. Under no circumstances will any legal liability or blame be held against the publisher for any reparation, damages, or monetary loss due to the information herein, either directly or indirectly.

Respective authors own all copyrights not held by the publisher.

Legal Notice:

This book is copyright protected. This is only for personal use. You cannot amend, distribute, sell, use, quote or paraphrase any part of the content within this book without the consent of the author or copyright owner. Legal action will be pursued if this is breached.

Disclaimer Notice:

Please note the information contained within this document is for educational and entertainment purposes only. Every attempt has been made to provide accurate, up-to-date and reliable, complete information. No warranties of any kind are expressed or implied. Readers acknowledge that the author is not engaging in the rendering of legal, financial, medical or professional advice.

By reading this document, the reader agrees that under no circumstances are we responsible for any losses, direct or indirect, which are incurred as a result of the use of information contained within this document, including, but not limited to, errors, omissions, or inaccuracies.

Table of contents

Introduction 6
Chapter 1: Understanding the Diabetes 7
    How to Identify If You Have Diabetes 7
    Types of Diabetes 8
    Risks of Type 2 Diabetes 9
    The Link Between Obesity and Type 2 Diabetes 9
    How Can Diabetes Be Prevented and Controlled 10
    A Healthy Meal Can Help Ease the Effects of Diabetes 10
    Food to Eat 10
    Food to Avoid 12
Chapter 2: Why Meal Prep 15
    The Benefits of Meal Prep 15
    How Do You Meal Prep and Eat Healthily 15
    How Long Does Food Stay Good When You Are Meal Prep? 16
Chapter 3: Breakfast Recipes 17
    Strawberry & Spinach Smoothie 17
    Quinoa Porridge 18
    Millet Porridge 19
    Bell Pepper Pancakes 20
    Sweet Potato Waffles 21
    Quinoa Bread 22
    Tofu Scramble 23
    Apple Omelet 24
    Veggie Frittata 25
    Chicken & Sweet Potato Hash 26
Chapter 4: Meat Recipes 27
    Beef Salad 27
    Beef Curry 29
    Beef with Barley & Veggies 31
    Beef with Broccoli 32
    Pan Grilled Steak 33
    Lamb Stew 34
    Lamb Curry 36
    Meatballs in Tomato Gravy 38
    Spiced Leg of Lamb 40

Baked Lamb & Spinach	42
Pork Salad	44
Pork with Bell Peppers	45
Roasted Pork Shoulder	46
Pork Chops in Peach Glaze	47
Ground Pork with Spinach	49

Chapter 5: Poultry Recipes 50

Chicken Soup	50
Chicken Chili	52
Chicken with Chickpeas	54
Chicken & Broccoli Bake	56
Meatballs Curry	57
Chicken, Oats & Chickpeas Meatloaf	59
Herbed Turkey Breast	61
Turkey with Lentils	62

Chapter 6: Vegetarian Recipes 64

Baked Beans	64
Spicy Black Beans	66
Lentils Chili	68
Quinoa in Tomato Sauce	70
Grains Combo	71
Barley Pilaf	72
Baked Veggies Combo	74
Mixed Veggie Salad	75
Tofu with Brussels Sprout	77
Beans, Walnuts & Veggie Burgers	78

Chapter 7: Sides Recipes 80

Spicy Spinach	80
Herbed Asparagus	81
Lemony Brussels Sprout	82
Gingered Cauliflower	83
Roasted Broccoli	84
Garlicky Cabbage	85
Stir Fried Zucchini	86
Green Beans with Tomatoes	87

Chapter 8: Fish & Seafood Recipes 88

Tuna Salad	88

Herring & Veggies Soup	89
Salmon Soup	90
Salmon & Shrimp Stew	91
Salmon Curry	93
Salmon with Bell Peppers	95
Shrimp Salad	96
Shrimp & Veggies Curry	98
Shrimp with Zucchini	99
Shrimp with Broccoli	100
Chapter 9: Dessert Recipes	**101**
Frozen Vanilla Yogurt	101
Spinach Sorbet	102
Avocado Mousse	103
Strawberry Mousse	104
Blueberries Pudding	105
Raspberry Chia Pudding	106
Brown Rice Pudding	107
Lemon Cookies	108
Yogurt Cheesecake	109
Conclusion	**110**

Introduction

The 2014 World Health Organization's report regarding Diabetes has shown that the number of diabetic patients around the world has increased from 4.6 percent in 1980 to 8.5 percent in 2014. These figures clearly reveal that this health deteriorating disease despite all the medical advancement has been on the rise. It is mainly because diabetes is not a pathogenic disease rather it is a result of body malfunction. Such an ailment is backed by number of factors including genetics, diet, environment, and lifestyle. Once a person is inflicted with Diabetes there can be no instant treatment to the problem except that we prevent its negative effects on the body by regulating the blood glucose levels. Diet control has been seen as the most effective method for such regulations, so, in this book we shall discover the basics of this Diabetic diet along with suitable low carb recipes. Another feature of this cookbook, which makes it interesting for all the diabetic dieters is that it gives you variety meal prep ideas so that you can easily cook and preserve healthy food conveniently.

Chapter 1: Understanding the Diabetes

How to Identify If You Have Diabetes

Whenever we here about Diabetes, lack of insulin production comes in mind. That is mainly because insulin is the hormone that enables the blood sugar to be absorbed and used by the cells and organs in the body. Its lack of production can raise the blood sugar levels while depriving the body of the glucose it actually needs. Insulin works to counter the effect of glucagon- another hormone that releases the sugar into the blood. In the absence of insulin, glucagon continues to work, and it can lead to more complications. When such a state persists, it is known as diabetes. There are different causes of diabetes, which shall be discussed in the next section. Here we shall see how a person can himself identify if he is suffering from diabetes silently. The following symptoms are common among all diabetic patients.

1. Frequent Urination

A marked disturbance in the blood sugar level directly affects the functioning of the kidney. To maintain its internal concentration balance, more water is released out of the body. It leads to frequent urination. This condition also leads to dehydration of the body and the skin.

2. Excessive Thirst

When water is constantly released out of the body, it will lead to excessive thirst. A person may need to consume more water to meet his liquid needs. All diabetic patients commonly deal with this problem.

3. Weight loss

Weight loss is not concerning in itself, but a sudden or abrupt weight loss is! This indicates that the body is depriving of vital nutrients and its energy needs are not met. This sign is not healthy, and the person should immediately consult a health expert.

4. Vision

High blood sugar levels indirectly affect the brain nerve cells, especially the optic nerves, and weakens the muscles of the eye controlling the lens. As a result, the vision is greatly affected, and it can be noticed within weeks of developing diabetes.

5. Numbness of limbs

The sensation in the hands and feet is great lost when you are suffering from diabetes. This is the reason many diabetic patients don't even feel pain in most parts of the body when hurt. This numbness can get into the way of the normal function of the hands and feet.

6. Hunger Pangs

Since the cells remain deprived of glucose, they constantly generate signals to indicate this deprivation. As a result, a person may suddenly feel hungry. It leads to unwanted cravings.

7. Fatigue

Fatigue is related to many chronic health disorders. It is also common among diabetic patients. They pretty much same the exhaustion all the time, even after rest. Get yourself check if that is the case.

8. Blood Sugar Levels

After noticing all the above-given symptoms, the last step is to confirm by checking the blood glucose levels. Normally a person has 70 to 130 mg/dL blood glucose. If this amount increases persistently, the person must be suffering from diabetes. Once the beta cells are damaged in the pancreas, they don't get to repair easily. That is why diabetes can only be controlled, and it can't be treated.

Types of Diabetes

1. Type I: Diabetes Miletus

This type of diabetes is developed as a body's own autoimmune response which means that this mechanism damages the pancreatic cells which produce insulin hormone. Resultantly, the pancreas simply stops producing required amount of insulin. It can occur at any age, no what your gender and genetic makeup are. People who suffer from diabetes type I require insulin to be injected from external sources daily basis in order to control blood glucose levels. They can also take it orally.

2. Type II: Insulin Resistance

The majority of diabetic patients suffer from this specific type of diabetes. It is usually diagnosed in adults, but sometimes in young adults too. This type of diabetes can remain undetected at early stages as it can only be identified properly through blood tests. A good diet plan and regular exercise can only control the negative effects of this diabetes. The patient may need some dose of insulin through medications. It is also termed as the 'Prediabetes,' and it is occurred due to the body's inability to react to the insulin normally produced by the body. The beta cells start producing more insulin as a result, and ultimate, they get exhausted or even damaged to an extent where they can no longer produce sufficient insulin.

3. Gestational diabetes (GDM)

This type of diabetes can develop in a mother during her gestational period or pregnancy. Well, it is not permanent but a temporary state and exists only during the pregnancy. It occurs due to the production of especial hormones from the placenta of the baby, and these hormones then affect the functioning and production of the insulin. So, the mother's body turns insulin resistant.

Risks of Type 2 Diabetes

Many risk factors are responsible for causing type II diabetes. It mainly develops due to the inactive lifestyle, sugar-rich diet, obesity, genetics, and environmental factors. However, if it persists the diseases can lead to whole new problems which appear to be far more complicated. Those conditions may include:

- Weight gain.
- High cholesterol levels
- High blood pressure.
- Nerve damage
- Kidney damage
- Sleep disorders
- Eye damage
- Polycystic ovarian syndrome

The Link Between Obesity and Type 2 Diabetes

3 out of every 5 patients of diabetes type II are obese around the world. This indicates that the rate of occurrence of insulin resistance in obese individuals is greater than the rest. Insulin resistance, in turn, then cause more obesity, and the cycle continues. Why exactly obesity causes insulin resistance? The fat deposited in the cells is mainly responsible for turning them insensitive towards insulin. It is partly because of the chemicals released through fat cells. The greater the deposition, the higher the chances of diabetes type II. The first thing that recommends to patients of insulin resistance is to control their weight or reduce it if necessary.

How Can Diabetes Be Prevented and Controlled

"Prevention is indeed better than cure," and that holds to be true for diabetes. As once it is developed the reversal seems quite difficult or next to impossible for some people. What comes next is just the control and maintenance of blood sugar levels so it would not cause any organ damage and other health complications. There are two methods to control the blood glucose: By increasing the amount of available insulin or controlling the spikes in blood sugar levels.

In the first method the insulin is injected into the person either orally or through injections so that it could lower the blood sugar levels. Even when insulin is consumed, a person should care for his diet. The other method is to control this sugar level by controlling the diet, by improving the rate of metabolism, and by leading an active lifestyle. These are natural means to curb the problem and leave more satisfying and long-lasting effects. This is why experts now suggest to use them as primary tool to deal with diabetes along sideline medications.

A Healthy Meal Can Help Ease the Effects of Diabetes

Food which can elevate the blood sugar level is primarily damaging for diabetic patients. A diet specially designed to remove all the ingredients potentially dangerous for diabetic patients can prove to be effective in easing its effects. Following are the food items which can be freely consumed on a Diabetic Diet:

Food to Eat

1. Vegetables

There is exactly no harm in adding veggies to your platter. The more, the better in fact. Except few exceptions, all vegetables are good for diabetic diets, such as:
- Spinach
- Broccoli
- Cauliflower
- Tomatoes
- Lemons
- Artichoke
- Garlic
- Asparagus
- Spring onions
- Onions
- Ginger etc.

2. Meat

Seafood is preferable for diabetic patients as it does not carry any amount of saturated fats. Then comes poultry can be consumed in moderation.
- All fish, i.e., salmon, halibut, trout, cod, sardine, etc.
- Mussels
- Shrimp
- Oysters
- Scallops
- Poultry

3. Fruits
- Strawberries
- Peaches
- Avocados
- Apples
- Kiwi Fruit
- Nectarines
- Berries
- Grapefruit
- Bananas
- Cherries
- Grapes
- Orange
- Pears
- Plums

4. Nuts and Seeds
- Sunflower seeds
- Pistachios
- Walnuts
- Pecans
- Pumpkin seeds
- Peanuts
- Almonds
- Sesame seeds

5. Grains
- Oats

- Quinoa
- Whole grains
- Tapioca
- Multigrain
- Brown rice
- Millet
- Sorghum
- Barley

6. Fats

- Olive oil
- Sesame oil
- Grapeseed oil
- Fats from plant sources

7. Diary

- Low-fat cheese
- Low-fat or fat-free Yogurt
- Skimmed milk
- Eggs
- Trans fat-free butter

8. Sugar Alternatives

Use the following low carb sweeteners wise and consider their taste and intensity of sweetness before adding them to the food of your choice.

- Xylitol
- Monk fruit
- Stevia
- Natvia
- Swerve
- Erythritol

Food to Avoid

Following food items can cause a spike in blood sugar levels and can indirectly aggravate the diabetic condition of a patient. Therefore, following ingredients should not be used in any amount on a Diabetic Diet.

1. All Sugars

- White sugar
- Brown sugar
- Confectionary sugar
- Honey
- Molasses
- Granulated sugar

2. High-Fat Products

When you are diabetic, you may get vulnerable to a number of fatal diseases like cardiovascular diseases. That is why doctors strictly forbid high-fat food products especially those sourced from dairy items. The high amount of fat can cause insulin resistance.

3. Saturated Fats

Saturated animal fats are never healthy for anyone, whether a diabetic patient or a normal individual. Whenever we are cooking meat, we should cut off all the excess fats. Cooking oils made out of saturated or trans fats should also be avoided. Distance yourself from all fat of animal origins.

4. High Carb Veggies

Vegetables that are high in starch are not suitable for diabetes. These veggies are responsible for increasing the carbohydrate levels of the food. So, avoid using them in the recipes and enjoy the other vegetables. Following are some of the high carb vegetables which should be avoided on this diet:

- Potatoes
- Yams

5. High Sodium Items

A high sodium diet can lead to hypertension and blood pressure. As diabetes is already caused by hormonal imbalance in the body, excess sodium can cause another imbalance- the fluid imbalance – which a diabetic body cannot bear. It further complicates the diseases. So, it is better to avoid using food, which is high in sodium. Mainly packed and processed foods and salt contain high dose of sodium. Use only the food products marked as 'Unsalted,' whether its margarine, nuts, butter, or other items.

6. Sugar- Rich Beverages

Cola drinks or other beverages are full of sugars. These drinks can drastically increase the blood glucose level within 30-40 minutes of drinking. Luckily, there are other sugar-free varieties in drinks available which are suitable for diabetic patients

7. High Cholesterol Items

Bad cholesterol or HDL - High-density Lipoprotein can deposit in different parts of the body and obstructs the flow of blood and the regulation of hormones. That is why food items having high bad cholesterol are not good for diabetes. Such items should be replaced with the ones with low cholesterol.

8. Sugar Mixed Syrups and Toppings

There are several syrups available in the markets which are full of sugar like Maple syrup, chocolate syrups, etc. A diabetic patient should avoid those sugary syrups and also stay away from the sugar-mixed toppings available in the stores.

9. Chocolate and Candies

Diabetic patients should use sugar-free chocolates or candies. Other processed bars and candies are extremely hazardous for their health, and all of such items should be avoided. You can try homemade low carb candies.

10. NO Alcohol

Alcohol can Now, reduce the rate of metabolism and can negatively affect appetite, which can lead to a very life-threatening situation for a diabetic patient. Excessive use of alcohol is damaging for the patients as it can excite the glucose levels in the blood.

Chapter 2: Why Meal Prep

The concept of meal prepping revolves around time and food management. It is the outcome of our health and diet concerns in this every busy lifestyle. The meal prep gives you an option to cook whenever convenient and store for later use. This technique can save a person from number of the dietary problems that are common in this age.

The Benefits of Meal Prep

Meal prepping offers the following benefits to every dieter:

1. Saves Time

Cooking every other day requires most of our time and effort. Rare are the people who can enjoy the luxury of time at this age. So, cooking the food for an entire week or more in a single day and saving it smartly can save a lot of our time and efforts.

2. Cost-Effective

One of the most obvious benefits of meal prepping is that it is very cost-effective. It is quite cheap to cook your own food than to order all the time due to lack of time. A person can easily manage his expenses when is cooking his own food.

3. Sets Direction

This is especially beneficial for all the dieters who gradually deviate from their path. When you plan your meal for an entire week and cook according to your dietary demands and limitation, you make sure to stick to the dietary plan. Very few chances are left for the last-minute change of mind.

4. Healthy Diet

When you keep a close eye on what you are eating and have even cooked and planned in your free time, then you would automatically set your preferences straight. A person would choose healthy food over everything. Nothing can be as healthy as eating home cooked meals at the right time.

How Do You Meal Prep and Eat Healthily

Meal prepping brings organization to your eating habits and put everything into the right order. With effective meal prepping strategies, a person can enjoy flavorsome healthy food with good nutrients. The following are the important steps to effective meal prepping.

1. Plan the Schedule

Based on your daily routine and your food needs and the specific diet plan, which is the diabetic diet in the current case, plan your menu first. Make the list of the recipes for the week or for the next three days or as desired. Set up your pantry first and fill it up accordingly. It is probably best to plan and cook during the weekend when you are free at home. Make sure the food is properly cooked.

2. Use Clean containers

Once it is cooked, it has to be packed tightly into airtight containers. Since air contains contamination, it can spoil the food inside. Always use clean and sanitize containers for this purpose otherwise all your efforts will go in vain.

3. Label the food

It is very important to label the food with its name and the day and time of serving. It will help to understand how much reheating temperature to be set and the number of servings etc.

4. Preserve Accordingly

Once the food is safely packed, it should be stored in the freezer. For a longer duration, freezing is the most effective technique. But if you are storing the food for the very next day then you can store it in the refrigerator.

5. Careful reheating

Over-reheating, or repeated reheating or even delayed reheating may spoil the taste of your food. It is therefore advised to heat the food accordingly. Avoid reheating at extremely high temperatures.

How Long Does Food Stay Good When You Are Meal Prep?

To answer this question, a person must keep three things in mind:

- Method of preservation
- Preservation tools
- And the timing of preservation

Sometimes people put all their efforts into cooking the meal, but when it comes to storing it, they turn negligent. If you preserve food in a loosely tight container that is not sanitized, the chances are the food will be spoiled the very next day. Similarly, if you store it in the refrigerator for more than 2 days, the food will also be spoiled. The experts suggest that food can stay good when stored in the freezer for a week at minimum of up to 2 weeks at maximum. Storing longer than this duration is not considered good for health. Similarly, when the food stored in the refrigerator can stay good for 2-3 days.

Chapter 3: Breakfast Recipes

Strawberry & Spinach Smoothie

Preparation Time: 10 minutes
Servings: 2

Ingredients:

- 1½ cups fresh strawberries, hulled and sliced
- 2 cups fresh baby spinach
- ½ cup fat-free plain Greek yogurt
- 1 cup unsweetened almond milk
- ¼ cup ice cubes

Method:

1. In a high-speed blender, add all the ingredients and pulse until smooth.
2. Pour into serving glasses and serve immediately.

Meal Prep Tip: In 2 zip lock bags, divide the strawberries and spinach. Seal the bags and store in the freezer for about 2-3 days. Just before serving, remove from the freezer and transfer into a blender with yogurt, almond milk and ice cubes and pulse until smooth.

Nutritional Value:

- Calories 96
- Total Fat 2.3 g
- Saturated Fat 0.2 g
- Cholesterol 1 mg
- Total Carbs 12.3 g
- Sugar 7.7 g
- Fiber 3.9 g
- Sodium 144 mg
- Potassium 428 mg
- Protein 8.1 g

Quinoa Porridge

Preparation Time: 10 minutes
Cooking Time: 15 minutes
Servings: 4

Ingredients:

- 2 cups water
- 1 cup dry quinoa, rinsed
- ½ teaspoon organic vanilla extract
- ½ cup unsweetened almond milk
- 10-12 drops liquid stevia
- ¼ teaspoon lemon peel, grated freshly
- ½ teaspoon ground cinnamon
- ½ teaspoon ground nutmeg
- Pinch of ground cloves
- 1 cup fresh mixed berries

Method:

1. In a pan, mix together the water, quinoa and vanilla essence over low heat and cook for about 15 minutes, stirring occasionally.
2. Stir in the almond milk, stevia, lemon peel and spices and immediately, remove from the heat.
3. Top with the berries and serve warm.

Meal Prep Tip: Transfer the cooled porridge in an airtight container and preserve in the refrigerator for up to 2 days. Just before serving, reheat in the microwave. Serve with the topping of berries.

Nutritional Value:

- Calories 186
- Total Fat 3.3 g
- Saturated Fat 0.4 g
- Cholesterol 0 mg
- Total Carbs 32.3 g
- Sugar 2.7 g
- Fiber 4.6 g
- Sodium 25 mg
- Potassium 312 mg
- Protein 6.4 g

Millet Porridge

Preparation Time: 10 minutes
Cooking Time: 25 minutes
Servings: 4

Ingredients:

- 1 cup millet, rinsed and drained
- Pinch of salt
- 3 cups water
- 2 tablespoons almonds, chopped finely
- 6-8 drops liquid stevia
- 1 cup unsweetened almond milk
- 2 tablespoons fresh blueberries

Method:

1. In a nonstick pan, add the millet over medium-low heat and cook for about 3 minutes, stirring continuously.
2. Add the salt and water and stir to combine
3. Increase the heat to medium and bring to a boil.
4. Cook for about 15 minutes.
5. Stir in the almonds, stevia and almond milk and cook for 5 minutes.
6. Top with the blueberries and serve.

Meal Prep Tip: Transfer the cooled porridge in an airtight container and preserve in the refrigerator for up to 2 days. Just before serving, reheat in the microwave. Serve with the topping of berries.

Nutritional Value:

- Calories 219
- Total Fat 4.5 g
- Saturated Fat 0.6 g
- Cholesterol 0 mg
- Total Carbs 38.2 g
- Sugar 0.6 g
- Fiber 5 g
- Sodium 92 mg
- Potassium 1721 mg
- Protein 6.4 g

Bell Pepper Pancakes

Preparation Time: 15 minutes
Cooking Time: 8 minutes
Servings: 2

Ingredients:

- ½ cup chickpea flour
- ¼ teaspoon baking powder
- Pinch of sea salt
- Pinch of red pepper flakes, crushed
- ½ cup plus 2 tablespoons filtered water
- ¼ cup green bell peppers, seeded and chopped finely
- ¼ cup scallion, chopped finely
- 2 teaspoons olive oil

Method:

1. In a bowl, mix together flour, baking powder, salt and red pepper flakes.
2. Add the water and mix until well combined.
3. Fold in bell pepper and scallion.
4. In a large frying pan, heat the oil over low heat.
5. Add half of the mixture and cook for about 1-2 minutes per side.
6. Repeat with the remaining mixture.
7. Serve warm.

Meal Prep Tip: Store these cooled pancakes into an airtight container by placing a piece of wax paper between each pancake. Refrigerate up to 4 days. Reheat in the microwave for about 1½-2 minutes.

Nutritional Value:

- Calories 232
- Total Fat 7.8 g
- Saturated Fat 1 g
- Cholesterol 0 mg
- Total Carbs 32.7 g
- Sugar 6.4 g
- Fiber 9.3 g
- Sodium 132 mg
- Potassium 566 mg
- Protein 10 g

Sweet Potato Waffles

Preparation Time: 10 minutes
Cooking Time: 20 minutes
Servings: 2

Ingredients:

- 1 medium sweet potato, peeled, grated and squeezed
- 1 teaspoon fresh thyme, minced
- 1 teaspoon fresh rosemary, minced
- 1/8 teaspoon red pepper flakes, crushed
- Salt and ground black pepper, as required

Method:

1. Preheat the waffle iron and then grease it.
2. In a large bowl, add all ingredients and mix till well combined.
3. Place half of the sweet potato mixture into preheated waffle iron and cook for about 8-10 minutes or until golden brown.
4. Repeat with the remaining mixture.
5. Serve warm.

Meal Prep Tip: Store these cooled waffles into an airtight container by placing a piece of wax paper between each waffle. Refrigerate up to 5 days. Reheat in the microwave for about 1-2 minutes.

Nutritional Value:

- Calories 72
- Total Fat 0.3 g
- Saturated Fat 0.1 g
- Cholesterol 0 mg
- Total Carbs 16.3 g
- Sugar 4.9 g
- Fiber 3 g
- Sodium 28 mg
- Potassium 369 mg
- Protein 1.6 g

Quinoa Bread

Preparation Time: 10 minutes
Cooking Time: 1½ hours
Servings: 12

Ingredients:

- 1¾ cups uncooked quinoa, rinsed, soaked overnight and drained
- ¼ cup chia seeds, soaked in ½ cup of water overnight
- ½ teaspoon bicarbonate soda
- Pinch of sea salt
- ½ cup filtered water
- ¼ cup olive oil, melted
- 1 tablespoon fresh lemon juice

Method:

1. Preheat the oven to 320 degrees F. Line a loaf pan with a parchment paper.
2. In a food processor, add all the ingredients and pulse for about 3 minutes.
3. Transfer the mixture into prepared loaf pan evenly.
4. Bake for about 1½ hours or until a wooden skewer inserted in the center of loaf comes out clean.
5. Remove the pan from oven and place onto a wire rack to cool for about 10-15 minutes.
6. Carefully, remove the bread from the loaf pan and place onto the wire rack to cool completely before slicing.
7. With a sharp knife, cut the bread loaf into desired sized slices and serve.

Meal Prep Tip: In a resealable plastic bag, place the bread and seal the bag after squeezing out the excess air. Set the bread away from direct sunlight and preserve in a cool and dry place for about 1-2 days.

Nutritional Value:

- Calories 137
- Total Fat 6.5 g
- Saturated Fat 0.9 g
- Cholesterol 0 mg
- Total Carbs 16.9 g
- Sugar 0 g
- Fiber 2.6 g
- Sodium 203 mg
- Potassium 158 mg
- Protein 4 g

Tofu Scramble

Preparation Time: 15 minutes
Cooking Time: 15 minutes
Servings: 2

Ingredients:

- ½ tablespoon olive oil
- 1 small onion, chopped finely
- 1 small red bell pepper, seeded and chopped finely
- 1 cup cherry tomatoes, chopped finely
- 1½ cups firm tofu, pressed and crumbled
- Pinch of ground turmeric
- Pinch of cayenne pepper
- 1 tablespoon fresh parsley, chopped

Method:

1. In a skillet, heat the oil over medium heat and sauté the onion and bell pepper for about 4-5 minute.
2. Add the tomatoes and cook for about 1-2 minutes.
3. Add the tofu, turmeric and cayenne pepper and cook for about 6-8 minutes.
4. Garnish with parsley and serve.

Meal Prep Tip: Transfer the cooled scramble into an airtight container and refrigerate for up to 3 days. Reheat in microwave before serving.

Nutritional Value:

- Calories 213
- Total Fat 11.8 g
- Saturated Fat 2.2 g
- Cholesterol 0 mg
- Total Carbs 14.7 g
- Sugar 8 g
- Fiber 4.5 g
- Sodium 31 mg
- Potassium 872 mg
- Protein 17.3 g

Apple Omelet

Preparation Time: 10 minutes
Cooking Time: 10 minutes
Servings: 3

Ingredients:

- 4 teaspoons olive oil, divided
- 2 small green apples, cored and sliced thinly
- ¼ teaspoon ground cinnamon
- Pinch of ground cloves
- Pinch of ground nutmeg
- 4 large eggs
- ¼ teaspoon organic vanilla extract
- Pinch of salt

Method:

1. In a large nonstick frying pan, heat 1 teaspoon of oil over medium-low heat.
2. Place the apple slices and sprinkle with spices.
3. Cook for about 4-5 minutes, flipping once halfway through.
4. Meanwhile, in a bowl, add the eggs, vanilla extract and salt and beat until fluffy.
5. Add the remaining oil in the pan and let it heat completely.
6. Place the egg mixture over apple slices evenly and cook for about 3-5 minutes or until desired doneness.
7. Carefully, turn the pan over a serving plate and immediately, fold the omelet.
8. Serve immediately.

Meal Prep Tip: In a resealable plastic bag, place the cooled omelet slices and seal the bag. Refrigerate for about 2-4 days. Reheat in the microwave on High for about 1 minute before serving.

Nutritional Value:

- Calories 228
- Total Fat 13.2 g
- Saturated Fat 3 g
- Cholesterol 248 mg
- Total Carbs 21.3 g
- Sugar 16.1 g
- Fiber 3.8 g
- Sodium 145 mg
- Potassium 251 mg
- Protein 8.8 g

Veggie Frittata

Preparation Time: 15 minutes
Cooking Time: 25 minutes
Servings: 6

Ingredients:

- 1 tablespoon olive oil
- 1 large sweet potato, peeled and cut into thin slices
- 1 yellow squash, sliced
- 1 zucchini, sliced
- ½ of red bell pepper, seeded and sliced
- ½ of yellow bell pepper, seeded and sliced
- 8 eggs
- Salt and ground black pepper, as required
- 2 tablespoons fresh cilantro, chopped finely

Method:

1. Preheat the oven to broiler.
2. In a large oven proof skillet, heat the oil over medium-low heat and cook the sweet potato for about 6-7 minutes.
3. Add the yellow squash, zucchini and bell peppers and cook for about 3-4 minutes.
4. Meanwhile, in a bowl, add the eggs, salt and black pepper and beat until well combined.
5. Pour egg mixture over vegetables mixture evenly.
6. Immediately, reduce the heat to low and cook for about 8-10 minutes or until just done.
7. Transfer the skillet in the oven and broil for about 3-4 minutes or until top becomes golden brown.
8. With a sharp knife, cut the frittata in desired size slices and serve with the garnishing of cilantro.

Meal Prep Tip: In a resealable plastic bag, place the cooled frittata slices and seal the bag. Refrigerate for about 2-4 days. Reheat in the microwave on High for about 1 minute before serving.

Nutritional Value:

- Calories 143
- Total Fat 8.4 g
- Saturated Fat 2.2 g
- Cholesterol 218 mg
- Total Carbs 9.3 g
- Sugar 4.2 g
- Fiber 1.1 g
- Sodium 98 mg
- Potassium 408 mg
- Protein 8.9 g

Chicken & Sweet Potato Hash

Preparation Time: 15 minutes
Cooking Time: 35 minutes
Servings: 8

Ingredients:

- 2 tablespoons olive oil, divided
- 1½ pounds boneless, skinless chicken breasts, cubed
- Salt and ground black pepper, as required
- 2 celery stalks, chopped
- 1 medium white onion, chopped
- 4 garlic cloves, minced
- 1 tablespoon fresh oregano, chopped
- 1 tablespoon fresh thyme, chopped
- 2 large sweet potatoes, peeled and cubed
- 1 cup low-sodium chicken broth
- 1 cup scallion, chopped
- 2 tablespoons fresh lime juice

Method:

1. In a large skillet, heat 1 tablespoon of oil over medium heat and cook the chicken with a little salt and black pepper for about 4-5 minutes.
2. Transfer the chicken into a bowl.
3. In the same skillet, heat the remaining oil over medium heat and sauté celery and onion for about 3-4 minutes.
4. Add the garlic and herbs and sauté for about 1 minute.
5. Add the sweet potato and cook for about 8-10 minutes.
6. Add the broth and cook for about 8-10 minutes.
7. Add the cooked chicken and scallion and cook for about 5 minutes.
8. Stir in lemon juice, salt and serve.

Meal Prep Tip: Transfer the cooled hash in an airtight container and preserve in the refrigerator for up to 2 days. Just before serving, reheat in the microwave.

Nutritional Value:

- Calories 253
- Total Fat 10 g
- Saturated Fat 2.3 g
- Cholesterol 76 mg
- Total Carbs 14 g
- Sugar 1.2 g
- Fiber 2.6 g
- Sodium 92 mg
- Potassium 597 mg
- Protein 26 g

Chapter 4: Meat Recipes

Beef Salad

Preparation Time: 20 minutes
Cooking Time: 8 minutes
Servings: 6

Ingredients:

For Steak:

- 1½ pounds skirt steak, trimmed and cut into 4 pieces
- Salt and ground black pepper, as required

For Salad:

- 2 medium green bell pepper, seeded and sliced thinly
- 2 large tomatoes, sliced
- 1 cup onion, sliced thinly
- 8 cups mixed fresh baby greens

For Dressing:

- 2 teaspoons Dijon mustard
- 4 tablespoons balsamic vinegar
- ½ cup olive oil
- Salt and ground black pepper, as required

Method:

1. Preheat the grill to medium-high heat. Grease the grill grate.
2. Sprinkle the beef steak with a little salt and black pepper.
3. Place the steak onto the grill and cook, covered for about 3-4 minutes per side.
4. Transfer the steak onto a cutting board for about 10 minutes before slicing.
5. With a sharp knife, cut the beef steaks into thin slices.
6. Meanwhile, in a large bowl, mix together all salad ingredients.
7. For dressing: in another bowl, add all the ingredients and beat until well combined.
8. Pour the dressing over salad and gently toss to coat well.
9. Divide the salad onto serving plates evenly.
10. Top each plate with the steak slices and serve.

Meal Prep Tip: In a small, jar, place the dressing. In 4 containers, divide salad and steak slices. Refrigerate the containers and jar of dressing for about 1 day. Just before serving, place the dressing over the salad and toss to coat well.

Nutritional Value:

- Calories 313
- Total Fat 21.4 g
- Saturated Fat 5.1 g
- Cholesterol 50 mg
- Total Carbs 6.4 g
- Sugar 3.4 g
- Fiber 1.7 g
- Sodium 88 mg
- Potassium 443mg
- Protein 24 g

Beef Curry

Preparation Time: 20 minutes
Cooking Time: 40 minutes
Servings: 6

Ingredients:

- 1 cup fat-free plain Greek yogurt
- ½ teaspoon garlic paste
- ½ teaspoon ginger paste
- ½ teaspoon ground cloves
- ½ teaspoon ground cumin
- 2 teaspoons red pepper flakes, crushed
- ¼ teaspoon ground turmeric
- Salt, as required
- 2 pounds round steak, cut into pieces
- ¼ cup olive oil
- 1 medium yellow onion, thinly sliced
- 1½ tablespoons fresh lemon juice
- ¼ cup fresh cilantro, chopped

Method:

1. In a large bowl, add the yogurt, garlic paste, ginger paste and spices and mix well.
2. Add the steak pieces and generously coat with the yogurt mixture.
3. Set aside for at least 15 minutes.
4. In a large skillet, heat the oil over medium-high heat and sauté the onion for about 4-5 minutes.
5. Add the steak pieces with marinade and stir to combine.
6. Immediately, adjust the heat to low and simmer, covered and cook for about 25 minutes, stirring occasionally.
7. Stir in the lemon juice and simmer for about 10 more minutes.
8. Garnish with fresh cilantro and serve hot.

Meal Prep Tip: Transfer the curry into a large bowl and set aside to cool. Divide the curry into 6 containers evenly. Cover the containers and refrigerate for 1-2 days. Reheat in the microwave before serving.

Nutritional Value:

- Calories 389
- Total Fat 18.2 g

- Saturated Fat 4.8 g
- Cholesterol 136 mg
- Total Carbs 4.3 g
- Sugar 2.4 g
- Fiber 0.7 g
- Sodium 149 mg
- Potassium 666 mg
- Protein 50.3 g

Beef with Barley & Veggies

Preparation Time: 15 minutes
Cooking Time: 1 hour 5 minutes
Servings: 2

Ingredients:

- ¾ cup filtered water
- ¼ cup pearl barley
- 2 teaspoons olive oil
- 7 ounces lean ground beef
- 1 cup fresh mushrooms, sliced
- ¾ cup onion, chopped
- 2 cups frozen green beans
- ¼ cup low-sodium beef broth
- 2 tablespoon fresh parsley, chopped

Method:

1. In a pan, add water, barley and pinch of salt and bring to a boil over medium heat.
2. Now, reduce the heat to low and simmer, covered for about 30-40 minutes or until all the liquid is absorbed.
3. Remove from heat and set aside.
4. In a skillet, heat oil over medium-high heat and cook beef for about 8-10 minutes.
5. Add the mushroom and onion and cook f or about 6-7 minutes.
6. Add the green beans and cook for about 2-3 minutes.
7. Stir in cooked barley and broth and cook for about 3-5 minutes more.
8. Stir in the parsley and serve hot.

Meal Prep Tip: Transfer the beef mixture into a large bowl and set aside to cool. Divide the mixture into 2 containers evenly. Cover the containers and refrigerate for 1-2 days. Reheat in the microwave before serving.

Nutritional Value:

- Calories 374
- Total Fat 11.4 g
- Saturated Fat 3.1 g
- Cholesterol 89 mg
- Total Carbs 32.7g
- Sugar 1.1 g
- Fiber 4.2 g
- Sodium 136 mg
- Potassium 895 mg
- Protein 36.6 g

Beef with Broccoli

Preparation Time: 10 minutes
Cooking Time: 14 minutes
Servings: 4

Ingredients:

- 2 tablespoons olive oil, divided
- 2 garlic cloves, minced
- 1-pound beef sirloin steak, trimmed and sliced into thin strips
- ¼ cup low-sodium chicken broth
- 2 teaspoons fresh ginger, grated
- 1 tablespoon ground flax seeds
- ½ teaspoon red pepper flakes, crushed
- Salt and ground black pepper, as required
- 1 large carrot, peeled and sliced thinly
- 2 cups broccoli florets
- 1 medium scallion, sliced thinly

Method:

1. In a large skillet, heat 1 tablespoon of oil over medium-high heat and sauté the garlic for about 1 minute.
2. Add the beef and cook for about 4-5 minutes or until browned.
3. With a slotted spoon, transfer the beef into a bowl.
4. Remove the excess liquid from skillet.
5. In a bowl, add the broth, ginger, flax seeds, red pepper flakes, salt and black pepper.
6. In the same skillet, heat remaining oil over medium heat.
7. Add the carrot, broccoli and ginger mixture and cook for about 3-4 minutes or until desired doneness.
8. Stir in beef and scallion and cook for about 3-4 minutes.

Meal Prep Tip: Transfer the beef mixture into a large bowl and set aside to cool. Divide the mixture into 4 containers evenly. Cover the containers and refrigerate for 1-2 days. Reheat in the microwave before serving.

Nutritional Value:

- Calories 211
- Total Fat 14.9 g
- Saturated Fat 3.9 g
- Cholesterol 101 mg
- Total Carbs 6.9 g
- Sugar 1.9 g
- Fiber 2.4 g
- Sodium 108 mg
- Potassium 706 mg
- Protein 36.5 g

Pan Grilled Steak

Preparation Time: 10 minutes
Cooking Time: 16 minutes
Servings: 4

Ingredients:

- 8 medium garlic cloves, crushed
- 1 (2-inch) piece fresh ginger, sliced thinly
- ¼ cup olive oil
- Salt and ground black pepper, as required
- 1½ pounds flank steak, trimmed

Method:

1. In a large sealable bag, mix together all ingredients except steak.
2. Add the steak and coat with marinade generously.
3. Seal the bag and refrigerate to marinate for about 24 hours.
4. Remove from refrigerator and keep in room temperature for about 15 minutes.
5. Discard the excess marinade from steak.
6. Heat a lightly greased grill pan over medium-high heat and cook the steak for about 6-8 minutes per side.
7. Remove from grill pan and set aside for about 10 minutes before slicing.
8. With a sharp knife cut into desired slices and serve.

Meal Prep Tip: Transfer the teak slices onto a wire rack to cool completely. With foil pieces, wrap the steak slices and refrigerate for about 1-2 days. Reheat in the microwave before serving.

Nutritional Value:

- Calories 447
- Total Fat 26.8 g
- Saturated Fat 7.7 g
- Cholesterol 94 mg
- Total Carbs 2.1g
- Sugar 0.1 g
- Fiber 0.2 g
- Sodium 96 mg
- Potassium 601 mg
- Protein 47.7 g

Lamb Stew

Preparation Time: 15 minutes
Cooking Time: 2¼ hours
Servings: 8

Ingredients:

- 1 teaspoon ground cumin
- 1 teaspoon ground coriander
- ½ teaspoon cayenne pepper
- ½ teaspoon ground cinnamon
- 2 tablespoons olive oil
- 3 pounds lamb stew meat, trimmed and cubed
- Sea Salt and ground black pepper, as required
- 1 onion, chopped
- 2 garlic cloves, minced
- 2¼ cups low-sodium chicken broth
- 2 cups tomatoes, chopped finely
- 1 medium head cauliflower, cut into 1-inch florets

Method:

1. Preheat the oven to 300 degrees F.
2. In a small bowl, mix together spices and set aside.
3. In a large ovenproof pan, heat oil over medium heat and cook the lamb with a little salt and black pepper for about 10 minutes or until browned from all sides.
4. With a slotted spoon, transfer the lamb into a bowl.
5. In the same pan, add onion and sauté for about 3-4 minutes.
6. Add the garlic and spice mixture and sauté for about 1 minute.
7. Add the cooked lamb, broth and tomatoes and bring to a gentle boil.
8. Immediately, cover the pan and transfer into oven.
9. Bake for about 1½ hours.
10. Remove from oven and stir in cauliflower.
11. Bake for about 30 minutes more or until cauliflower is done completely.
12. Serve hot.

Meal Prep Tip: Transfer the stew into a large bowl and set aside to cool. Divide the stew into 8 containers evenly. Cover the containers and refrigerate for 1-2 days. Reheat in the microwave before serving.

Nutritional Value:

- Calories 375
- Total Fat 16.2 g
- Saturated Fat 5 g
- Cholesterol 153 mg
- Total Carbs 5.6 g
- Sugar 2.6 g
- Fiber 1.8 g
- Sodium 162 mg
- Potassium 808 mg
- Protein 49.7 g

Lamb Curry

Preparation Time: 15 minutes
Cooking Time: 2¼ hours
Servings: 8

Ingredients:

For Spice Mixture:

- 2 teaspoons ground coriander
- 2 teaspoons ground cumin
- 1 teaspoon ground cinnamon
- ½ teaspoon ground ginger
- 1 tablespoon sweet paprika
- ½ tablespoon cayenne pepper
- 1 teaspoon red chili powder
- Salt and ground black pepper, as required

For Curry:

- 1 tablespoon olive oil
- 2 pounds boneless lamb, trimmed and cubed into 1-inch size
- 2 cups onions, chopped
- ½ cup fat-free plain Greek yogurt, whipped
- 1½ cups water

Method:

1. For spice mixture: in a bowl, add all spices and mix well. Set aside.
2. In a large Dutch oven, heat the oil over medium-high heat and stir fry the lamb cubes for about 5 minutes.
3. Add the onion and cook for about 4-5 minutes.
4. Stir in the spice mixture and cook for about 1 minute.
5. Add the yogurt and water and bring to a boil over high heat.
6. Now, reduce the heat to low and simmer, covered for about 1-2 hours or until desired doneness of lamb.
7. Uncover and simmer for about 3-4 minutes.
8. Serve hot.

Meal Prep Tip: Transfer the curry into a large bowl and set aside to cool. Divide the curry into 8 containers evenly. Cover the containers and refrigerate for 1-2 days. Reheat in the microwave before serving.

Nutritional Value:
- Calories 254
- Total Fat 10.5 g
- Saturated Fat 3.3 g
- Cholesterol 102 mg
- Total Carbs 4.7 g
- Sugar 1.9 g
- Fiber 1.4 g
- Sodium 99 mg
- Potassium 468 mg
- Protein 34 g

Meatballs in Tomato Gravy

Preparation Time: 20 minutes
Cooking Time: 30 minutes
Servings: 6

Ingredients:

For Meatballs:

- 1-pound lean ground lamb
- 1 tablespoon homemade tomato paste
- ¼ cup fresh cilantro leaves, chopped
- 1 small onion, chopped finely
- 2 garlic cloves, minced
- ½ teaspoon ground cumin
- 1/8 teaspoon salt
- Ground black pepper, as required

For Tomato Gravy:

- 3 tablespoons olive oil, divided
- 2 medium onions, chopped finely
- 2 garlic cloves, minced
- ½ tablespoon fresh ginger, minced
- 1 teaspoon dried thyme, crushed
- 1 teaspoon dried oregano, crushed
- 3 large tomatoes, chopped finely
- Ground black pepper, as required
- 1½ cups warm low-sodium chicken broth

Method:

1. For meatballs: in a large bowl, add all the ingredients and mix until well combined.
2. Make small equal-sized balls from mixture and set aside.
3. For gravy: in a large pan, heat 1 tablespoon of oil over medium heat.
4. Add the meatballs and cook for about 4-5 minutes or until lightly browned from all sides.
5. With a slotted spoon, transfer the meatballs onto a plate.
6. In the same pan, heat the remaining oil over medium heat and sauté the onion for about 8-10 minutes.
7. Add the garlic, ginger and herbs and sauté for about 1 minute.

8. Add the tomatoes and cook for about 3-4 minutes, crushing with the back of spoon.
9. Add the warm broth and bring to a boil.
10. Carefully, place the meatballs and cook for 5 minutes, without stirring.
11. Now, reduce the heat to low and cook partially covered for about 15-20 minutes, stirring gently 2-3 times.
12. Serve hot.

Meal Prep Tip: Transfer the meatballs mixture into a large bowl and set aside to cool. Divide the mixture into 6 containers evenly. Cover the containers and refrigerate for 1-2 days. Reheat in the microwave before serving.

Nutritional Value:

- Calories 248
- Total Fat 12.9 g
- Saturated Fat 3 g
- Cholesterol 68 mg
- Total Carbs 10 g
- Sugar 4.8 g
- Fiber 2.5 g
- Sodium 138 mg
- Potassium 591 mg
- Protein 23.4 g

Spiced Leg of Lamb

Preparation Time: 15 minutes
Cooking Time: 1 hour 40 minutes
Servings: 6

Ingredients:

For Marinade:

- 2/3 cup fat-free plain Greek yogurt
- 1 tablespoon homemade tomato puree
- 1 tablespoon fresh lemon juice
- 3-4 garlic cloves, minced
- 2 tablespoons fresh rosemary, chopped
- 2 teaspoons ground coriander
- 1 teaspoon ground cumin
- 1 teaspoon ground cinnamon
- 1 teaspoon red pepper flakes, crushed
- ¼ teaspoon sweet paprika
- Sea salt and freshly ground black pepper, as required
- 1 (4½-pound) bone-in leg of lamb

Method:

1. In a large bowl, add yogurt, tomato puree, lemon juice, garlic, rosemary, and spices and mix until well combined.
2. Add leg of lamb and coat with marinade generously.
3. Cover and refrigerate to marinate for about 8-10 hours, flipping occasionally.
4. Remove the marinated leg of lamb from refrigerator and keep in room temperature for about 25-30 minutes before roasting.
5. Preheat the oven to 425-degree F.
6. Line a large roasting pan with a greased foil piece.
7. Arrange the leg of lamb into prepared roasting pan.
8. Roast for 20 minutes.
9. Remove the roasting pan from oven and change the side of leg of lamb.
10. Now, Now, reduce the temperature of oven to 325-degree F.
11. Roast for 40 minutes.
12. Now loosely cover the roasting pan with a large piece of foil.
13. Roast for 40 minutes more.

14. Remove from oven and place onto a cutting board for about 10-15 minutes before slicing.
15. With a sharp knife cut the leg of lamb in desired sized slices and serve.

Meal Prep Tip: Transfer the leg slices onto a wire rack to cool completely. With foil pieces, wrap the leg slices and refrigerate for about 1-2 days. Reheat in the microwave before serving.

Nutritional Value:

- Calories 478
- Total Fat 15.5 g
- Saturated Fat 6.1 g
- Cholesterol 226 mg
- Total Carbs 3.3 g
- Sugar 1.3 g
- Fiber 0.9 g
- Sodium 226 mg
- Potassium 48 mg
- Protein 72.3 g

Baked Lamb & Spinach

Preparation Time: 15 minutes
Cooking Time: 2 hours 55 minutes
Servings: 6

Ingredients:

- 2 tablespoons olive oil
- 2 pounds lamb necks, trimmed and cut into 2-inch pieces crosswise
- Salt, as required
- 2 medium onions, chopped
- 3 tablespoons fresh ginger, minced
- 4 garlic cloves, minced
- 2 tablespoons ground coriander
- 1 tablespoon ground cumin
- 1 teaspoon ground turmeric
- ¼ cup fat-free plain Greek yogurt
- ½ cup tomatoes, chopped
- 2 cups boiling water
- 30 ounces frozen spinach, thawed and squeezed
- 1½ tablespoons garam masala
- 1 tablespoon fresh lemon juice
- Ground black pepper, as required

Method:

1. Preheat the oven to 300 degrees F.
2. In a large Dutch oven, heat the oil over medium-high heat and stir fry the lamb necks with a little salt for about 4-5 minutes or until browned completely.
3. With a slotted spoon, transfer the lamb onto a plate and Now, reduce the heat to medium.
4. In the same pan, add the onion and sauté for about 10 minutes.
5. Add the ginger, garlic and spices and sauté for about 1 minute.
6. Add the yogurt and tomatoes and cook for about 3-4 minutes.
7. With an immersion blender, blend the mixture until smooth.
8. Add the lamb, boiling water and salt and bring to a boil.
9. Cover the pan and transfer into the oven.
10. Bake for about 2½ hours.
11. Now, remove the pan from oven and place over medium heat.
12. Stir in spinach and garam masala and cook for about 3-5 minutes.

13. Stir in lemon juice, salt and black pepper and remove from heat.
14. Serve hot.

Meal Prep Tip: Transfer the lamb mixture into a large bowl and set aside to cool. Divide the mixture into 6 containers evenly. Cover the containers and refrigerate for 1-2 days. Reheat in the microwave before serving.

Nutritional Value:

- Calories 469
- Total Fat 32.4 g
- Saturated Fat 13.4 g
- Cholesterol 0 mg
- Total Carbs 12.9 g
- Sugar 3.1 g
- Fiber 4.7 g
- Sodium 304 mg
- Potassium 957 mg
- Protein 34.1 g

Pork Salad

Preparation Time: 15 minutes
Cooking Time: 6 minutes
Servings: 5

Ingredients:

- 1½ pounds pork tenderloin, trimmed and sliced thinly
- Salt and ground black pepper, as required
- 3 tablespoon olive oil
- 2 carrots, peeled and grated
- 3 cups Napa cabbage, shredded
- 2 scallions, chopped
- 2 tablespoon fresh lime juice
- ¼ cup fresh mint leaves, chopped

Method:

1. Season the pork with salt and black pepper lightly.
2. In a large skillet, heat the oil over medium heat and cook the pork slices for about 2-3 minutes per sides or until cooked through.
3. Remove from the heat and set aside to cool slightly.
4. In a large bowl, add the pork and remaining ingredients except mint leaves and toss to coat well.
5. Serve with the garnishing of mint leaves.

Meal Prep Tip: In 5 containers, divide salad. Refrigerate the containers for about 1 day. Just before serving, stir the salad well.

Nutritional Value:

- Calories 292
- Total Fat 13.3 g
- Saturated Fat 2.9 g
- Cholesterol 99 mg
- Total Carbs 5.7 g
- Sugar 2.7 g
- Fiber 2.1 g
- Sodium 104 mg
- Potassium 760 mg
- Protein 36.6 g

Pork with Bell Peppers

Preparation Time: 15 minutes
Cooking Time: 13 minutes
Servings: 4

Ingredients:

- 1 tablespoon fresh ginger, chopped finely
- 4 garlic cloves, chopped finely
- 1 cup fresh cilantro, chopped and divided
- ¼ cup plus 1 tablespoon olive oil, divided
- 1-pound tender pork, trimmed, sliced thinly
- 2 onions, sliced thinly
- 1 green bell pepper, seeded and sliced thinly
- 1 red bell pepper, seeded and sliced thinly
- 1 tablespoon fresh lime juice

Method:

1. In a large bowl, mix together ginger, garlic, ½ cup of cilantro and ¼ cup of oil.
2. Add the pork and coat with mixture generously.
3. Refrigerate to marinate for about 2 hours.
4. Heat a large skillet over medium-high heat and stir fry the pork mixture for about 4-5 minutes.
5. Transfer the pork into a bowl.
6. In the same skillet, heat remaining oil over medium heat and sauté the onion for about 3 minutes.
7. Stir in the bell pepper and stir fry for about 3 minutes.
8. Stir in the pork, lime juice and remaining cilantro and cook for about 2 minutes.
9. Serve hot.

Meal Prep Tip: Transfer the pork mixture into a large bowl and set aside to cool. Divide the mixture into 4 containers evenly. Cover the containers and refrigerate for 1-2 days. Reheat in the microwave before serving.

Nutritional Value:

- Calories 360
- Total Fat 21.8 g
- Saturated Fat 3.9 g
- Cholesterol 83 mg
- Total Carbs 11 g
- Sugar 5.4 g
- Fiber 2.2 g
- Sodium 71 mg
- Potassium 706 mg
- Protein 31.2 g

Roasted Pork Shoulder

Preparation Time: 10 minutes
Cooking Time: 6 hours
Servings: 12

Ingredients:

- 1 head garlic, peeled and crushed
- ¼ cup fresh rosemary, minced
- 2 tablespoons fresh lemon juice
- 2 tablespoons balsamic vinegar
- 1 (4-pound) pork shoulder, trimmed

Method:

1. In a bowl, add all the ingredients except pork shoulder and mix well.
2. In a large roasting pan place pork shoulder and coat with marinade generously.
3. With a large plastic wrap, cover the roasting pan and refrigerate to marinate for at least 1-2 hours.
4. Remove the roasting pan from refrigerator.
5. Remove the plastic wrap from roasting pan and keep in room temperature for 1 hour.
6. Preheat the oven to 275 degrees F.
7. Arrange the roasting pan in oven and roast for about 6 hours.
8. Remove from the oven and set aside for about 15-20 minutes.
9. With a sharp knife, cut the pork shoulder into desired slices and serve.

Meal Prep Tip: Transfer the pork slices onto a wire rack to cool completely. With foil pieces, wrap the pork slices and refrigerate for about 1-2 days. Reheat in the microwave before serving.

Nutritional Value:

- Calories 450
- Total Fat 32.6g
- Saturated Fat 12 g
- Cholesterol 136 mg
- Total Carbs 1.5 g
- Sugar 0.1 g
- Fiber 0.6 g
- Sodium 104 mg
- Potassium 522 mg
- Protein 35.4 g

Pork Chops in Peach Glaze

Preparation Time: 15 minutes
Cooking Time: 16 minutes
Servings: 2

Ingredients:

- 2 (6-ounce) boneless pork chops, trimmed
- Sea Salt and ground black pepper, as required
- ½ of ripe yellow peach, peeled, pitted and chopped
- 1 tablespoon olive oil
- 2 tablespoons shallot, minced
- 2 tablespoons garlic, minced
- 2 tablespoons fresh ginger, minced
- 4-6 drops liquid stevia
- 1 tablespoon balsamic vinegar
- ¼ teaspoon red pepper flakes, crushed
- ¼ cup filtered water

Method:

1. Season the pork chops with sea salt and black pepper generously.
2. In a blender, add the peach pieces and pulse until a puree form.
3. Reserve the remaining peach pieces.
4. In a skillet, heat the oil over medium heat and sauté the shallots for about 1-2 minutes.
5. Add the garlic and ginger and sauté for about 1 minute.
6. Stir in the remaining ingredients and bring to a boil.
7. Now, reduce the heat to medium-low and simmer for about 4-5 minutes or until a sticky glaze form.
8. Remove from the heat and reserve 1/3 of the glaze and set aside.
9. Coat the chops with remaining glaze.
10. Heat a nonstick skillet over medium-high heat and sear the chops for about 4 minutes per side.
11. Transfer the chops onto a plate and coat with the remaining glaze evenly.
12. Serve immediately.

Meal Prep Tip: Transfer the pork chops into a large bowl and set aside to cool. Divide the chops into 2 containers evenly. Cover the containers and refrigerate for 1-2 days. Reheat in the microwave before serving.

Nutritional Value:
- Calories 359
- Total Fat 13.5 g
- Saturated Fat 3.2 g
- Cholesterol 124 mg
- Total Carbs 12 g
- Sugar 3.8 g
- Fiber 1.5 g
- Sodium 102 mg
- Potassium 938 mg
- Protein 46.2 g

Ground Pork with Spinach

Preparation Time: 15 minutes
Cooking Time: 15 minutes
Servings: 4

Ingredients:

- 1 tablespoon olive oil
- ½ of white onion, chopped
- 2 garlic cloves, chopped finely
- 1 jalapeño pepper, chopped finely
- 1-pound lean ground pork
- 1 teaspoon ground coriander
- 1 teaspoon ground cumin
- ½ teaspoon ground turmeric
- ½ teaspoon ground cinnamon
- ½ teaspoon ground fennel seeds
- Salt and ground black pepper, as required
- ½ cup fresh cherry tomatoes, quartered
- 1¼ pounds collard greens leaves, stemmed and chopped
- 1 teaspoon fresh lemon juice

Method:

1. In a large skillet, heat the oil over medium heat and sauté the onion for about 4 minutes.
2. Add the garlic and jalapeño pepper and sauté for about 1 minute.
3. Add the pork and spices and cook for about 6 minutes breaking into pieces with the spoon.
4. Stir in the tomatoes and greens and cook, stirring gently for about 4 minutes.
5. Stir in the lemon juice and remove from heat.
6. Serve hot.

Meal Prep Tip: Transfer the pork mixture into a large bowl and set aside to cool. Divide the mixture into 4 containers evenly. Cover the containers and refrigerate for 1-2 days. Reheat in the microwave before serving.

Nutritional Value:

- Calories 316
- Total Fat 21.8 g
- Saturated Fat 0.5 g
- Cholesterol 0 mg
- Total Carbs 11.4 g
- Sugar 1.4 g
- Fiber 5.7 g
- Sodium 27 mg
- Potassium 107 mg
- Protein 23 g

Chapter 5: Poultry Recipes

Chicken Soup

Preparation Time: 15 minutes
Cooking Time: 23 minutes
Servings: 4

Ingredients:

- 1 tablespoon olive oil
- 1 small carrot, peeled and chopped
- ½ cup onion, chopped
- 1 celery stalk, chopped
- 2 garlic cloves, minced
- 1 tablespoon fresh thyme, chopped
- 1 tablespoon fresh rosemary, chopped
- ½ teaspoon ground cumin
- ¼ teaspoon red pepper flakes, crushed
- 5 cups low-sodium chicken broth
- 1¼ cups cooked chicken, chopped
- 2 cups fresh spinach, torn
- 1¼ cups zucchini, chopped
- Ground black pepper, as required
- 2 tablespoons fresh lime juice
- 1 teaspoon fresh lime zest, grated finely

Method:

1. In a large soup pan, heat the oil over medium heat and sauté the carrot, onion and celery for about 8-9 minutes.
2. Add the garlic, rosemary and spices and sauté for about 1 minute.
3. Add the broth and bring to a boil over high heat.
4. Now, reduce the heat to medium-low and simmer for about 5 minutes.
5. Add the cooked chicken, spinach and zucchini and simmer for about 6-8 minutes.
6. Stir in the black pepper and lime juice and remove from heat.
7. Serve hot with the garnishing of lime zest.

Meal Prep Tip: Transfer the soup into a large bowl and set aside to cool. Divide the soup into 4 containers evenly. Cover the containers and refrigerate for 1-2 days. Reheat in the microwave before serving.

Nutritional Value:
- Calories 224
- Total Fat 6.8g
- Saturated Fat 1.4 g
- Cholesterol 74 mg
- Total Carbs 7.5 g
- Sugar 2 g
- Fiber 2.2 g
- Sodium 178 mg
- Potassium 456 mg
- Protein 31.8 g

Chicken Chili

Preparation Time: 15 minutes
Cooking Time: 40 minutes
Servings: 6

Ingredients:

- 4 cups low-sodium chicken broth, divided
- 3 cups boiled black beans, divided
- 1 tablespoon extra-virgin olive oil
- 1 large onion, chopped
- 1 jalapeño pepper, seeded and chopped
- 4 garlic cloves, minced
- 1 teaspoon dried thyme, crushed
- 1½ tablespoons ground coriander
- 1 tablespoon ground cumin
- ½ tablespoon red chili powder
- 4 cups cooked chicken, shredded
- 1 tablespoon fresh lime juice
- ¼ cup fresh cilantro, chopped

Method:

1. In a food processor, add 1 cup of broth and 1 can of black beans and pulse until smooth.
2. Transfer the beans puree into a bowl and set aside.
3. In a large pan, heat the oil over medium heat and sauté the onion and jalapeño for about 4-5 minutes.
4. Add the garlic, spices and sea salt and sauté for about 1 minute.
5. Add the beans puree and remaining broth and bring to a boil.
6. Now, reduce the heat to low and simmer for about 20 minutes.
7. Stir in the remaining can of beans, chicken and lime juice and bring to a boil.
8. Now, reduce the heat to low and simmer for about 5-10 minutes.
9. Serve hot with the garnishing of cilantro.

Meal Prep Tip: Transfer the chili into a large bowl and set aside to cool. Divide the chili into 6 containers evenly. Cover the containers and refrigerate for 1-2 days. Reheat in the microwave before serving.

Nutritional Value:

- Calories 356
- Total Fat 7.1 g
- Saturated Fat 1.2 g
- Cholesterol 72 mg
- Total Carbs 33 g
- Sugar 2.7 g
- Fiber 11.6 g
- Sodium 130 mg
- Potassium 662 mg
- Protein 39.6 g

Chicken with Chickpeas

Preparation Time: 15 minutes
Cooking Time: 36 minutes
Servings: 4

Ingredients:

- 2 tablespoons olive oil
- 1-pound skinless, boneless chicken breast, cubed
- 2 carrots, peeled and sliced
- 1 onion, chopped
- 2 celery stalks, chopped
- 2 garlic cloves, chopped
- 1 tablespoon fresh ginger root, minced
- ½ teaspoon dried oregano, crushed
- ¾ teaspoon ground cumin
- ½ teaspoon paprika
- ¼-13 teaspoon cayenne pepper
- ¼ teaspoon ground turmeric
- 1 cup tomatoes, crushed
- 1½ cups low-sodium chicken broth
- 1 zucchini, sliced
- 1 cup boiled chickpeas, drained
- 1 tablespoon fresh lemon juice

Method:

1. In a large nonstick pan, heat the oil over medium heat and cook the chicken cubes for about 4-5 minutes.
2. With a slotted spoon, transfer the chicken cubes onto a plate.
3. In the same pan, add the carrot, onion, celery and garlic and sauté for about 4-5 minutes.
4. Add the ginger, oregano and spices and sauté for about 1 minute.
5. Add the chicken, tomato and broth and bring to a boil.
6. Now, reduce the heat to low and simmer for about 10 minutes.
7. Add the zucchini and chickpeas and simmer, covered for about 15 minutes.
8. Stir in the lemon juice and serve hot.

Meal Prep Tip: Transfer the chicken mixture into a large bowl and set aside to cool. Divide the mixture into 4 containers evenly. Cover the containers and refrigerate for 1-2 days. Reheat in the microwave before serving.

Nutritional Value:

- Calories 308
- Total Fat 12.3 g
- Saturated Fat 2.7 g
- Cholesterol 66 mg
- Total Carbs 19 g
- Sugar 5.3g
- Fiber 4.7 g
- Sodium 202 mg
- Potassium 331 mg
- Protein 30.7 g

Chicken & Broccoli Bake

Preparation Time: 15 minutes
Cooking Time: 45 minutes
Servings: 6

Ingredients:

- 6 (6-ounce) boneless, skinless chicken breasts
- 3 broccoli heads, cut into florets
- 4 garlic cloves, minced
- ¼ cup olive oil
- 1 teaspoon dried oregano, crushed
- 1 teaspoon dried rosemary, crushed
- Sea Salt and ground black pepper, as required

Method:

1. Preheat the oven to 375 degrees F. Grease a large baking dish.
2. In a large bowl, add all the ingredients and toss to coat well.
3. In the bottom of prepared baking dish, arrange the broccoli florets and top with chicken breasts in a single layer.
4. Bake for about 45 minutes.
5. Remove from the oven and set aside for about 5 minutes before serving.

Meal Prep Tip: Remove the baking dish from the oven and set aside to cool completely. In 6 containers, divide the chicken breasts and broccoli evenly and refrigerate for about 2 days. Reheat in microwave before serving.

Nutritional Value:

- Calories 443
- Total Fat 21.5 g
- Saturated Fat 4.7 g
- Cholesterol 151 mg
- Total Carbs 9.4 g
- Sugar 2.2g
- Fiber 3.6 g
- Sodium 189 mg
- Potassium 831 mg
- Protein 53 g

Meatballs Curry

Preparation Time: 20 minutes
Cooking Time: 25 minutes
Servings: 6

Ingredients:

For Meatballs:

- 1-pound lean ground chicken
- 1 tablespoon onion paste
- 1 teaspoon fresh ginger paste
- 1 teaspoons garlic paste
- 1 green chili, chopped finely
- 1 tablespoon fresh cilantro leaves, chopped
- 1 teaspoon ground coriander
- ½ teaspoon cumin seeds
- ½ teaspoon red chili powder
- ½ teaspoon ground turmeric
- 1/8 teaspoon salt

For Curry:

- 3 tablespoons olive oil
- ½ teaspoon cumin seeds
- 1 (1-inch) cinnamon stick
- 2 onions, chopped
- 1 teaspoon fresh ginger, minced
- 1 teaspoons garlic, minced
- 4 tomatoes, chopped finely
- 2 teaspoons ground coriander
- 1 teaspoon garam masala powder
- ½ teaspoon ground nutmeg
- ½ teaspoon red chili powder
- ½ teaspoon ground turmeric
- Salt, as required
- 1 cup filtered water
- 3 tablespoons fresh cilantro, chopped

Method:

1. For meatballs: in a large bowl, add all ingredients and mix until well combined.
2. Make small equal-sized meatballs from mixture.
3. In a large deep skillet, heat the oil over medium heat and cook the meatballs for about 3-5 minutes or until browned from all sides.
4. Transfer the meatballs into a bowl.
5. In the same skillet, add the cumin seeds and cinnamon stick and sauté for about 1 minute.
6. Add the onions and sauté for about 4-5 minutes.
7. Add the ginger and garlic paste and sauté for about 1 minute.
8. Add the tomato and spices and cook, crushing with the back of spoon for about 2-3 minutes.
9. Add the water and meatballs and bring to a boil.
10. Now, reduce the heat to low and simmer for about 10 minutes.
11. Serve hot with the garnishing of cilantro.

Meal Prep Tip: Transfer the curry into a large bowl and set aside to cool. Divide the curry into 5 containers evenly. Cover the containers and refrigerate for 1-2 days. Reheat in the microwave before serving.

Nutritional Value:

- Calories 196
- Total Fat 11.4 g
- Saturated Fat 2.4 g
- Cholesterol 53 mg
- Total Carbs 7.9 g
- Sugar 3.9 g
- Fiber 2.1 g
- Sodium 143 mg
- Potassium 279 mg
- Protein 16.7 g

Chicken, Oats & Chickpeas Meatloaf

Preparation Time: 20 minutes
Cooking Time: 1¼ hours
Servings: 4

Ingredients:

- ½ cup cooked chickpeas
- 2 egg whites
- 2½ teaspoons poultry seasoning
- Ground black pepper, as required
- 10-ounce lean ground chicken
- 1 cup red bell pepper, seeded and minced
- 1 cup celery stalk, minced
- 1/3 cup steel-cut oats
- 1 cup tomato puree, divided
- 2 tablespoons dried onion flakes, crushed
- 1 tablespoon prepared mustard

Method:

1. Preheat the oven to 350 degrees F. Grease a 9x5-inch loaf pan.
2. In a food processor, add chickpeas, egg whites, poultry seasoning and black pepper and pulse until smooth.
3. Transfer the mixture into a large bowl.
4. Add the chicken, veggies oats, ½ cup of tomato puree and onion flakes and mix until well combined.
5. Transfer the mixture into prepared loaf pan evenly.
6. With your hands, press, down the mixture slightly.
7. In another bowl mix together mustard and remaining tomato puree.
8. Place the mustard mixture over loaf pan evenly.
9. Bake for about 1-1¼ hours or until desired doneness.
10. Remove from the oven and set aside for about 5 minutes before slicing.g.
11. Cut into desired sized slices and serve.

Meal Prep Tip: In a resealable plastic bag, place the cooled meatloaf slices and seal the bag. Refrigerate for about 2-4 days. Reheat in the microwave on High for about 1 minute before serving.

Nutritional Value:

- Calories 229
- Total Fat 5.6 g
- Saturated Fat 1.4 g
- Cholesterol 50 mg
- Total Carbs 23.7 g
- Sugar 5.2 g
- Fiber 4.7 g
- Sodium 227 mg
- Potassium 509 mg
- Protein 21.4 g

Herbed Turkey Breast

Preparation Time: 15 minutes
Cooking Time: 1 hour 50 minutes
Servings: 6

Ingredients:

- ½ cup olive oil
- 2 tablespoons fresh lemon juice
- 1 tablespoon scallion, chopped
- ½ teaspoon dried marjoram, crushed
- ½ teaspoon dried sage, crushed
- ½ teaspoon dried thyme, crushed
- Salt and ground black pepper, as required
- 1 (2-pound) boneless, skinless turkey breast half

Method:

1. Preheat the oven to 325 degrees F. Arrange a rack into a greased shallow roasting pan.
2. In a small pan, all the ingredients except turkey breast over medium heat and bring to a boil, stirring frequently.
3. Remove from the heat and set aside to cool.
4. Place turkey breast into the prepared roasting pan.
5. Place some of the herb mixture over the top of turkey breast.
6. Cover the roasting pan and bake for about 1¼-1¾ hours, basting with the remaining herb mixture occasionally.
7. Remove from the oven and set aside for about 10-15 minutes before slicing.
8. With a sharp knife, cut into desired slices and serve.

Meal Prep Tip: Transfer the turkey breast slices onto a wire rack to cool completely. With foil pieces, wrap the turkey breast slices and refrigerate for about 1-2 days. Reheat in the microwave before serving.

Nutritional Value:

- Calories 319
- Total Fat 17.5 g
- Saturated Fat 2.4 g
- Cholesterol 93 mg
- Total Carbs 0.3 g
- Sugar 0.1 g
- Fiber 0.1 g
- Sodium 75 mg
- Potassium 45 mg
- Protein 27.4 g

Turkey with Lentils

Preparation Time: 15 minutes
Cooking Time: 51 minutes
Servings: 7

Ingredients:

- 3 tablespoons olive oil, divided
- 1 onion, chopped
- 1 tablespoon fresh ginger, minced
- 4 garlic cloves, minced
- 3 plum tomatoes, chopped finely
- 2 cups dried red lentils, soaked for 30 minutes and drained
- 2 cups filtered water
- 2 teaspoons cumin seeds
- ½ teaspoon cayenne pepper
- 1-pound lean ground turkey
- 1 jalapeño pepper, seeded and chopped
- 2 scallions, chopped
- ¼ cup fresh cilantro, chopped

Method:

1. In a Dutch oven, heat 1 tablespoon of oil over medium heat and sauté the onion, ginger and garlic for about 5 minutes.
2. Stir in tomatoes, lentils and water and bring to a boil
3. Now, reduce the heat to medium-low and simmer, covered for about 30 minutes.
4. Meanwhile, in a skillet, heat remaining oil over medium heat and sauté the cumin seeds and cayenne pepper for about 1 minute.
5. Transfer the mixture into a small bowl and set aside.
6. In the same skillet, add turkey and cook for about 4-5 minutes.
7. Add the jalapeño and scallion and cook for about 4-5 minutes.
8. Add the spiced oil mixture and stir to combine well.
9. Transfer the turkey mixture in simmering lentils and simmer for about 10-15 minutes or until desired doneness.
10. Serve hot.

Meal Prep Tip: Transfer the turkey mixture into a large bowl and set aside to cool. Divide the mixture into 4 containers evenly. Cover the containers and refrigerate for 1-2 days. Reheat in the microwave before serving.

Nutritional Value:
- Calories 361
- Total Fat 11.5.4 g
- Saturated Fat 2.4 g
- Cholesterol 46 mg
- Total Carbs 37 g
- Sugar 3.4 g
- Fiber 18 g
- Sodium 937mg
- Potassium 331 mg
- Protein 27.9 g

Chapter 6: Vegetarian Recipes

Baked Beans

Preparation Time: 15 minutes
Cooking Time: 2 hours 10 minutes
Servings: 4

Ingredients:

- ¼ pound dry lima beans, soaked overnight and drained
- ¼ pound dry red kidney beans, soaked overnight and drained
- 1¼ tablespoons 0ive oil
- 1 small onion, chopped
- 4 garlic cloves, minced
- 1 teaspoon dried thyme, crushed
- ½ teaspoon ground cumin
- ½ teaspoon red pepper flakes, crushed
- ¼ teaspoon paprika
- 1 tablespoon balsamic vinegar
- 1 cup homemade tomato puree
- 1 cup low-sodium vegetable broth
- Ground black pepper, as required
- 2 tablespoons fresh parsley, chopped

Method:

1. In a large pan of the boiling water, add the beans over high heat and bring to a boil.
2. Now, reduce the heat to low and simmer, covered for about 1 hour.
3. Remove from the heat and drain the beans well.
4. Preheat the oven to 325 degrees F.
5. In a large ovenproof pan, heat the oil over medium heat and cook the onion for about 8-9 minutes, stirring frequently.
6. Add the garlic, thyme and red spices and sauté for about 1 minute.
7. Add the cooked beans and remaining ingredients and immediately remove from the heat.
8. Cover the pan and transfer into the oven.
9. Bake for about 1 hour.
10. Serve with the garnishing of cilantro.

Meal Prep Tip: Transfer the beans mixture into a large bowl and set aside to cool. Divide the mixture into 4 containers evenly. Cover the containers and refrigerate for 1-2 days. Reheat in the microwave before serving.

Nutritional Value:

- Calories 136
- Total Fat 4.3 g
- Saturated Fat 0.9 g
- Cholesterol 0 mg
- Total Carbs 19 g
- Sugar 4.7 g
- Fiber 4.6 g
- Sodium 112 mg
- Potassium 472 mg
- Protein 5.7 g

Spicy Black Beans

Preparation Time: 15 minutes
Cooking Time: 1½ hours
Servings: 6

Ingredients:

- 4 cups filtered water
- 1½ cups dried black beans, soaked for 8 hours and drained
- ½ teaspoon ground turmeric
- 3 tablespoons olive oil
- 1 small onion, chopped finely
- 1 green chili, chopped
- 1 (1-inch) piece fresh ginger, minced
- 2 garlic cloves, minced
- 1-1½ tablespoons ground coriander
- 1 teaspoon ground cumin
- ½ teaspoon cayenne pepper
- Sea salt, as required
- 2 medium tomatoes, chopped finely
- ½ cup fresh cilantro, chopped

Method:

1. In a large pan, add water, black beans and turmeric and bring to a boil on high heat.
2. Now, reduce the heat to low and simmer, covered for about 1 hour or till desired doneness of beans.
3. Meanwhile, in a skillet, heat the oil over medium heat and sauté the onion for about 4-5 minutes.
4. Add the green chili, ginger, garlic, spices and salt and sauté for about 1-2 minutes.
5. Stir in the tomatoes and cook for about 10 minutes, stirring occasionally.
6. Transfer the tomato mixture into the pan with black beans and stir to combine.
7. Increase the heat to medium-low and simmer for about 15-20 minutes.
8. Stir in the cilantro and simmer for about 5 minutes.
9. Serve hot.

Meal Prep Tip: Transfer the beans mixture into a large bowl and set aside to cool. Divide the mixture into 6 containers evenly. Cover the containers and refrigerate for 1-2 days. Reheat in the microwave before serving.

Nutritional Value:
- Calories 160
- Total Fat 8 g
- Saturated Fat 1 g
- Cholesterol 0 mg
- Total Carbs 17.9 g
- Sugar 2.4 g
- Fiber 6.2 g
- Sodium 50 mg
- Potassium 343 mg
- Protein 6 g

Lentils Chili

Preparation Time: 15 minutes
Cooking Time: 2 hours 20 minutes
Servings: 8

Ingredients:

- 2 teaspoons olive oil
- 1 large onion, chopped
- 3 medium carrot, peeled and chopped
- 4 celery stalks, chopped
- 2 garlic cloves, minced
- 1 jalapeño pepper, seeded and chopped
- ½ tablespoon dried thyme, crushed
- 1 tablespoon chipotle chili powder
- ½ tablespoon cayenne pepper
- 1½ tablespoons ground coriander
- 1½ tablespoons ground cumin
- 1 teaspoon ground turmeric
- Ground black pepper, as required
- 1 tomato, chopped finely
- 1-pound lentils, rinsed
- 8 cups low-sodium vegetable broth
- 6 cups fresh spinach
- ½ cup fresh cilantro, chopped

Method:

1. In a large pan, heat the oil over medium heat and sauté the onion, carrot and celery for about 5 minutes.
2. Add the garlic, jalapeño pepper, thyme and spices and sauté for about 1 minute.
3. Add the tomato paste, lentils and broth and bring to a boil.
4. Now, reduce the heat to low and simmer for about 2 hours.
5. Stir in the spinach and simmer for about 3-5 minutes.
6. Stir in cilantro and remove from the heat.
7. Serve hot.

Meal Prep Tip: Transfer the chili into a large bowl and set aside to cool. Divide the chili into 8 containers evenly. Cover the containers and refrigerate for 1-2 days. Reheat in the microwave before serving.

Nutritional Value:
- Calories 259
- Total Fat 2.3 g
- Saturated Fat 0.3 g
- Cholesterol 0 mg
- Total Carbs 41 g
- Sugar 3.6 g
- Fiber 19 g
- Sodium 118 mg
- Potassium 856 mg
- Protein 18.2 g

Quinoa in Tomato Sauce

Preparation Time: 15 minutes
Cooking Time: 40 minutes
Servings: 4

Ingredients:

- 2 tablespoons olive oil
- 1 cup quinoa, rinsed
- 1 green bell pepper, seeded and chopped
- 1 medium onion, chopped finely
- 3 garlic cloves, minced
- 2½ cups filtered water
- 2 cups tomatoes, crushed finely
- 1 teaspoon red chili powder
- ¼ teaspoon ground cumin
- ¼ teaspoon garlic powder
- Ground black pepper, as required

Method:

1. In a large pan, heat the oil over medium-high heat and cook the quinoa, onion, bell pepper and garlic for about 5 minutes, stirring frequently.
2. Stir in the remaining ingredients and bring to a boil.
3. Now, reduce the heat to medium-low.
4. Cover the pan tightly and simmer for about 30 minutes, stirring occasionally.
5. Serve hot.

Meal Prep Tip: Transfer the quinoa mixture into a large bowl and set aside to cool. Divide the chili into 4 containers evenly. Cover the containers and refrigerate for 1-2 days. Reheat in the microwave before serving.

Nutritional Value:

- Calories 260
- Total Fat 10 g
- Saturated Fat 1.4 g
- Cholesterol 0 mg
- Total Carbs 36.9 g
- Sugar 5.2 g
- Fiber 5.4 g
- Sodium 16 mg
- Potassium 575 mg
- Protein 7.7 g

Grains Combo

Preparation Time: 15 minutes
Cooking Time: 35 minutes
Servings: 6

Ingredients:

- ¾ cup amaranth
- 1 cup quinoa, rinsed
- ¼ cup wild rice
- 4¼ cups filtered water
- 2 teaspoons ground cumin
- ½ teaspoon paprika
- Salt, as required
- 1¼ cups boiled chickpeas
- 2 medium carrots, peeled and grated
- 1 garlic clove, minced
- Ground black pepper, as required

Method:

1. In a large pan, add the amaranth, quinoa, wild rice, water and spices over medium-high heat and bring to a boil.
2. Now, reduce the heat to medium-low and simmer, covered for about 20-25 minutes.
3. Stir in remaining ingredients and simmer for about 3-5 minutes.
4. Serve hot.

Meal Prep Tip: Transfer the grains mixture into a large bowl and set aside to cool. Divide the mixture into 6 containers evenly. Cover the containers and refrigerate for 1 day. Reheat in the microwave before serving.

Nutritional Value:

- Calories 365
- Total Fat 5.6 g
- Saturated Fat 0.6 g
- Cholesterol 0 mg
- Total Carbs 64 g
- Sugar 5.8 g
- Fiber 12 g
- Sodium 58 mg
- Potassium 686 mg
- Protein 16.4 g

Barley Pilaf

Preparation Time: 20 minutes
Cooking Time: 1 hour 5 minutes
Servings: 4

Ingredients:

- ½ cup pearl barley
- 1 cup low-sodium vegetable broth
- 2 tablespoons olive oil, divided
- 2 garlic cloves, minced finely
- ½ cup onion, chopped
- ½ cup eggplant, sliced thinly
- ½ cup green bell pepper, seeded and chopped
- ½ cup red bell pepper, seeded and chopped
- 2 tablespoons fresh cilantro, chopped
- 2 tablespoons fresh mint leaves, chopped

Method:

1. In a pan, add the barley and broth over medium-high heat and bring to a boil.
2. Immediately, reduce the heat to low and simmer, covered for about 45 minutes or until all the liquid is absorbed.
3. In a large skillet, heat 1 tablespoon of oil over high heat and sauté the garlic for about 1 minute.
4. Stir in the cooked barley and cook for about 3 minutes.
5. Remove from heat and set aside.
6. In another skillet, heat remaining oil over medium heat and sauté the onion for about 5-7 minutes.
7. Add the eggplant and bell peppers and stir fry for about 3 minutes.
8. Stir in the remaining ingredients except walnuts and cook for about 2-3 minutes.
9. Stir in barley mixture and cook for about 2-3 minutes.
10. Serve hot.

Meal Prep Tip: Transfer the pilaf into a large bowl and set aside to cool. Divide the pilaf into 4 containers evenly. Cover the containers and refrigerate for 1 day. Reheat in the microwave before serving.

Nutritional Value:

- Calories 168
- Total Fat 7.4 g

- Saturated Fat 1.1 g
- Cholesterol 0 mg
- Total Carbs 23.5 g
- Sugar 1.9 g
- Fiber 5 g
- Sodium 22 mg
- Potassium 164 mg
- Protein 3.6 g

Baked Veggies Combo

Preparation Time: 15 minutes
Cooking Time: 40 minutes
Servings: 8

Ingredients:

- 2 large zucchinis, sliced
- 1 large yellow squash, sliced
- 3 cups fresh broccoli florets
- 1-pound fresh asparagus, trimmed
- 2 garlic cloves, minced
- 1 tablespoon fresh rosemary, minced
- 1 tablespoon fresh thyme, minced
- ½ teaspoon ground cumin
- ½ teaspoon red pepper flakes, crushed
- ¼ teaspoon cayenne pepper
- 2 tablespoons olive oil
- Salt, as required

Method:

1. Preheat the oven to 400 degrees F. Line 2 large baking sheets with aluminum foil.
2. In a large bowl, add all ingredients and toss to coat well.
3. Divide the vegetables mixture onto prepared baking sheets and spread in a single layer.
4. Roast for about 35-40 minutes.
5. Remove from oven and serve.

Meal Prep Tip: Remove from oven and set the veggies aside to cool completely. Transfer the veggie mixture into 8 containers and refrigerate for 2-3 days. Reheat in microwave before serving.

Nutritional Value:

- Calories 77
- Total Fat 4 g
- Saturated Fat 0.6 g
- Cholesterol 0 mg
- Total Carbs 9.4 g
- Sugar 3.8 g
- Fiber 3.8 g
- Sodium 45 mg
- Potassium 554 mg
- Protein 3.8 g

Mixed Veggie Salad

Preparation Time: 20 minutes
Servings: 8

Ingredients:

For Dressing:

- 1/3 cup olive oil
- ½ cup fresh lemon juice
- 1 tablespoon fresh ginger, grated
- 2 teaspoons mustard
- 4-6 drops liquid stevia
- ¼ teaspoon salt

For Salad:

- 2 avocados, peeled, pitted and chopped
- 2 tablespoons fresh lemon juice
- 2 cups fresh baby spinach, torn
- 2 cups small broccoli florets
- 1 cup red cabbage, shredded
- 1 cup purple cabbage, shredded
- 2 large carrots, peeled and grated
- 1 small orange bell pepper, seeded and sliced into matchsticks
- 1 small yellow bell pepper, seeded and sliced into matchsticks
- ½ cup fresh parsley leaves, chopped
- 1 cup walnuts, chopped

Method:

1. For dressing: in a food processor, add all ingredients and pulse until well combined.
2. In a large bowl, add the avocado slices and drizzle with lemon juice.
3. Add the remaining vegetables and mix.
4. Place the dressing and toss to coat well.
5. Serve immediately.

Meal Prep Tip: Transfer dressing into a small jar and refrigerate for 1 day. In 8 containers, divide avocado and remaining vegetables. Refrigerate for 1 day. Before serving, drizzle each portion with dressing and serve.

Nutritional Value:
- Calories 314
- Total Fat 28.1 g
- Saturated Fat 4 g
- Cholesterol 0 mg
- Total Carbs 14.1 g
- Sugar 4.3g
- Fiber 6.9 g
- Sodium 113 mg
- Potassium 642 mg
- Protein 6.8 g

Tofu with Brussels Sprout

Preparation Time: 15 minutes
Cooking Time: 15 minutes
Servings: 4

Ingredients:

- 1 tablespoon olive oil, divided
- 8 ounces extra-firm tofu, drained, pressed and cut into slices
- 2 garlic cloves, chopped
- 1/3 cup pecans, toasted and chopped
- 1 tablespoon unsweetened applesauce
- ¼ cup fresh cilantro, chopped
- ¾ pound Brussels sprouts, trimmed and cut into wide ribbons

Method:

1. In a skillet, heat ½ tablespoon of the oil over medium heat and sauté the tofu and for about 6-7 minutes or until golden brown.
2. Add the garlic and pecans and sauté for about 1 minute.
3. Add the applesauce and cook for about 2 minutes.
4. Stir in the cilantro and remove from heat.
5. Transfer tofu into a plate and set aside.
6. In the same skillet, heat the remaining oil over medium-high heat and cook the Brussels sprouts for about 5 minutes.
7. Stir in the tofu and remove from the heat.
8. Serve immediately.

Meal Prep Tip: Remove the tofu mixture from heat and set aside to cool completely. In 4 containers, divide the tofu mixture evenly and refrigerate for about 2 days. Reheat in microwave before serving.

Nutritional Value:

- Calories 204
- Total Fat 15.5 g
- Saturated Fat 1.8 g
- Cholesterol 0 mg
- Total Carbs 11.5 g
- Sugar 3 g
- Fiber 4.8 g
- Sodium 27 mg
- Potassium 468 mg
- Protein 9.9 g

Beans, Walnuts & Veggie Burgers

Preparation Time: 20 minutes
Cooking Time: 25 minutes
Servings: 8

Ingredients:

- ½ cup walnuts
- 1 carrot, peeled and chopped
- 1 celery stalk, chopped
- 4 scallions, chopped
- 5 garlic cloves, chopped
- 2¼ cups cooked black beans
- 2½ cups sweet potato, peeled and grated
- ½ teaspoon red pepper flakes, crushed
- ¼ teaspoon cayenne pepper
- Salt and ground black pepper, as required

Method:

1. Preheat the oven to 400 degrees F. Line a baking sheet with parchment paper.
2. In a food processor, add walnuts and pulse until finely ground.
3. Add the carrot, celery, scallion and garlic and pulse until chopped finely.
4. Transfer the vegetable mixture into a large bowl.
5. In the same food processor, add beans and pulse until chopped.
6. Add 1½ cups of sweet potato and pulse until a chunky mixture form.
7. Transfer the bean mixture into the bowl with vegetable mixture.
8. Stir in the remaining sweet potato and spices and mix until well combined.
9. Make 8 patties from mixture.
10. Arrange the patties onto prepared baking sheet in a single layer.
11. Bake for about 25 minutes.
12. Serve hot.

Meal Prep Tip: Remove the burgers from oven and set aside to cool completely. Store these burgers in an airtight container, by placing parchment papers between the burgers to avoid the sticking. These burgers can be stored in the freezer for up to 3 weeks. Before serving, thaw the burgers and then reheat in microwave.

Nutritional Value:

- Calories 177
- Total Fat 5 g

- Saturated Fat 0.3 g
- Cholesterol 0 mg
- Total Carbs 27.6 g
- Sugar 5.3 g
- Fiber 7.6 g
- Sodium 205 mg
- Potassium 398 mg
- Protein 8 g

Chapter 7: Sides Recipes

Spicy Spinach

Preparation Time: 10 minutes
Cooking Time: 20 minutes
Servings: 3

Ingredients:

- 1 tablespoon olive oil
- 1 red onion, chopped finely
- 6 garlic cloves, minced
- 1 (1-inch) piece fresh ginger, minced
- 1 teaspoon garam masala
- 1 teaspoon ground coriander
- ½ teaspoon ground cumin
- ¼ teaspoon ground turmeric
- 6 cups fresh spinach, chopped
- Salt and ground black pepper, as required
- 1-2 tablespoons water

Method:

1. Heat the olive oil in a large nonstick skillet over medium heat and sauté the onion for about 6-7 minutes.
2. Add the garlic, ginger and spices and sauté for about 1 minute.
3. Add the spinach, salt and black pepper and water and cook, covered for about 10 minutes.
4. Uncover and stir fry for about 2 minutes.
5. Serve hot.

Meal Prep Tip: Transfer the spinach mixture into a large bowl and set aside to cool completely. Divide the mixture into 3 containers evenly. Cover the containers and refrigerate for about 1-2 days. Reheat in the microwave before serving.

Nutritional Value:

- Calories 80
- Total Fat 5.1 g
- Saturated Fat 0.7 g
- Cholesterol 0 mg
- Total Carbs 8 g
- Sugar 1.9 g
- Fiber 2.3 g
- Sodium 52 mg
- Potassium 331 mg
- Protein 2.6 g

Herbed Asparagus

Preparation Time: 10 minutes
Cooking Time: 10 minutes
Servings: 4

Ingredients:

- 2 tablespoons olive oil
- 2 tablespoons fresh lemon juice
- 1 tablespoon balsamic vinegar
- 1 teaspoon garlic, minced
- 1 tablespoon fresh parsley, chopped
- 1 teaspoon dried oregano
- Salt and ground black pepper, as required
- 1-pound fresh asparagus, ends removed

Method:

1. Preheat oven to 400 degrees F and lightly grease a rimmed baking sheet.
2. Place the oil, lemon juice, vinegar, garlic, herbs, salt and black pepper in a bowl and beat until well combined.
3. Arrange the asparagus onto the prepared baking sheet in a single layer.
4. Top with half of the herb mixture and toss to coat.
5. Roast for about 8-10 minutes.
6. Remove from the oven and transfer the asparagus onto a platter.
7. Drizzle with the remaining herb mixture and serve.

Meal Prep Tip: Transfer the asparagus into a large bowl and set aside to cool completely. Divide the asparagus into 4 containers evenly. Cover the containers and refrigerate for about 1-2 days. Reheat in the microwave before serving.

Nutritional Value:

- Calories 88
- Total Fat 7.3 g
- Saturated Fat 1.1 g
- Cholesterol 0 mg
- Total Carbs 5.1 g
- Sugar 2.4 g
- Fiber 2.6 g
- Sodium 5 mg
- Potassium 256 mg
- Protein 2.7 g

Lemony Brussels Sprout

Preparation Time: 10 minutes
Cooking Time: 7 minutes
Servings: 2

Ingredients:

- ½ pound Brussels sprouts, halved
- 1 tablespoon olive oil
- 1 garlic clove, minced
- ½ teaspoon red pepper flakes, crushed
- Salt and ground black pepper, as required
- 1 tablespoon fresh lemon juice

Method:

1. Heat the olive oil in a large skillet over medium heat and cook the garlic and red pepper flakes for about 1 minute, stirring continuously.
2. Stir in the Brussels sprouts, salt and black pepper and sauté for about 4-5 minutes.
3. Stir in lemon juice and sauté for about 1 minute more.
4. Serve hot.

Meal Prep Tip: Transfer the Brussels sprouts into a large bowl and set aside to cool completely. Divide the Brussels sprouts into 2 containers evenly. Cover the containers and refrigerate for about 1-2 days. Reheat in the microwave before serving.

Nutritional Value:

- Calories 114
- Total Fat 7.5 g
- Saturated Fat 1.2 g
- Cholesterol 0 mg
- Total Carbs 11.2 g
- Sugar 2.7 g
- Fiber 4.4 g
- Sodium 108 mg
- Potassium 465 mg
- Protein 4.1 g

Gingered Cauliflower

Preparation Time: 0 minutes
Cooking Time: 0 minutes
Servings: 2

Ingredients:

- 2 cups cauliflower, cut into 1-inch florets
- Salt, as required
- 2 tablespoons olive oil
- 1 teaspoon fresh ginger root, sliced thinly
- 2 fresh thyme sprigs

Method:

1. In a pan of the water, add the cauliflower and salt over medium heat and bring to a boil.
2. Cover and cook for about 10-12 minutes.
3. Drain the cauliflower well and transfer onto a serving platter.
4. Meanwhile, in a small skillet, melt the coconut oil over medium-low heat.
5. Add the ginger and thyme sprigs and swirl the pan occasionally for about 2-3 minutes.
6. Discard the ginger and thyme sprigs.
7. Pour the oil over cauliflower and serve immediately.

Meal Prep Tip: Transfer the cauliflower into a large bowl and set aside to cool completely. Divide the cauliflower into 2 containers evenly. Cover the containers and refrigerate for about 1-2 days. Reheat in the microwave before serving.

Nutritional Value:

- Calories 147
- Total Fat 14.2 g
- Saturated Fat 2 g
- Cholesterol 0 mg
- Total Carbs 5.7 g
- Sugar 2.4 g
- Fiber 2.7 g
- Sodium 108 mg
- Potassium 310 mg
- Protein 2 g

Roasted Broccoli

Preparation Time: 10 minutes
Cooking Time: 15 minutes
Servings: 2

Ingredients:

- 2 cups fresh broccoli florets
- 1 small yellow onion, cut into wedges
- ¼ teaspoon garlic powder
- 1/8 teaspoon paprika
- 1/8 teaspoon freshly ground black pepper
- 2 tablespoons olive oil

Method:

1. Preheat the grill to medium heat.
2. In a large bowl, add all the ingredients and toss to coat well.
3. Transfer the broccoli mixture over a double thickness of a foil paper.
4. Fold the foil paper around broccoli mixture to seal it.
5. Grill for about 10-15 minutes.
6. Serve hot.

Meal Prep Tip: Transfer the broccoli mixture into a large bowl and set aside to cool completely. Divide the broccoli mixture into 2 containers evenly. Cover the containers and refrigerate for about 1-2 days. Reheat in the microwave before serving.

Nutritional Value:

- Calories 167
- Total Fat 14.4 g
- Saturated Fat 2 g
- Cholesterol 0 mg
- Total Carbs 9.7 g
- Sugar 3.1 g
- Fiber 3.2 g
- Sodium 32 mg
- Potassium 348 mg
- Protein 3 g

Garlicky Cabbage

Preparation Time: 10 minutes
Cooking Time: 10 minutes
Servings: 4

Ingredients:

- 1 tablespoon olive oil
- 2 garlic cloves, minced
- 1-pound cabbage, shredded
- 2-3 tablespoons filtered water
- 1½ tablespoons fresh lemon juice
- Salt and ground black pepper, as required

Method:

1. In a large skillet, heat the oil over medium heat and sauté the garlic for about 1 minute.
2. Stir in the cabbage and cook, covered for about 2-3 minute.
3. Stir in the water and cook for about 2-3 minutes, stirring continuously.
4. Increase the heat to high and stir in the lemon juice, salt and black pepper.
5. Cook for about 2-3 minutes, stirring continuously.
6. Serve hot.

Meal Prep Tip: Transfer the cabbage mixture into a large bowl and set aside to cool completely. Divide the cabbage mixture into 2 containers evenly. Cover the containers and refrigerate for about 1-2 days. Reheat in the microwave before serving.

Nutritional Value:

- Calories 62
- Total Fat 3.7 g
- Saturated Fat 0.6 g
- Cholesterol 0 mg
- Total Carbs 7.2 g
- Sugar 3.8 g
- Fiber 2.9 g
- Sodium 168 mg
- Potassium 206 mg
- Protein 1.6 g

Stir Fried Zucchini

Preparation Time: 10 minutes
Cooking Time: 10 minutes
Servings: 4

Ingredients:

- 1 tablespoon olive oil
- ½ cup yellow onion, sliced
- 4 cups zucchini, sliced
- 1½ teaspoons garlic, minced
- ¼ cup water
- Salt and ground black pepper, as required

Method:

1. In a large skillet, heat the oil over medium-high heat and sauté the onion and zucchini for about 4-5 minutes.
2. Add the garlic and sauté for about 1 minute.
3. Add the remaining ingredients and stir to combine.
4. Now, reduce the heat to medium and cook for about 3-4 minutes, stirring occasionally.
5. Serve hot.

Meal Prep Tip: Transfer the zucchini mixture into a large bowl and set aside to cool completely. Divide the zucchini mixture into 4 containers evenly. Cover the containers and refrigerate for about 1-2 days. Reheat in the microwave before serving.

Nutritional Value:

- Calories 55
- Total Fat 3.7 g
- Saturated Fat 0.5 g
- Cholesterol 0 mg
- Total Carbs 5.5 g
- Sugar 2.6 g
- Fiber 1.6 g
- Sodium 51 mg
- Potassium 321 mg
- Protein 1.6 g

Green Beans with Tomatoes

Preparation Time: 15 minutes
Cooking Time: 40 minutes
Servings: 8

Ingredients:

- ¼ teaspoon fresh lemon peel, grated finely
- 2 teaspoons olive oil
- Salt and freshly ground white pepper, as required
- 4 cups grape tomatoes
- 1½ pounds fresh green beans, trimmed

Method:

1. Preheat the oven to 350 degrees F.
2. In a large bowl, mix together lemon peel, oil, salt and white pepper.
3. Add the cherry tomatoes and toss to coat well.
4. Transfer the tomato mixture into a roasting pan.
5. Roast for about 35-40 minutes, stirring once in the middle way.
6. Meanwhile, in a pan of boiling water, arrange a steamer basket.
7. Place the green beans in steamer basket and steam, covered for about 7-8 minutes.
8. Drain the green beans well.
9. Divide the green beans and tomatoes onto serving plates and serve.

Meal Prep Tip: Transfer the green beans and tomatoes into a large bowl and set aside to cool completely. Divide the green beans and tomatoes into 8 containers evenly. Cover the containers and refrigerate for about 1-2 days. Reheat in the microwave before serving.

Nutritional Value:

- Calories 53
- Total Fat 1.5 g
- Saturated Fat 0.2 g
- Cholesterol 0 mg
- Total Carbs 9.6 g
- Sugar 3.6 g
- Fiber 4 g
- Sodium 29 mg
- Potassium 391 mg
- Protein 2.3 g

Chapter 8: Fish & Seafood Recipes

Tuna Salad

Preparation Time: 15 minutes
Servings: 2

Ingredients:

- 2 (5-ounce) cans water packed tuna, drained
- 2 tablespoons fat-free plain Greek yogurt
- Salt and ground black pepper, as required
- 2 medium carrots, peeled and shredded
- 2 apples, cored and chopped
- 2 cups fresh spinach, torn

Method:

1. In a large bowl, add the tuna, yogurt, salt and black pepper and gently, stir to combine.
2. Add the carrots and apples and stir to combine.
3. Serve immediately.

Meal Prep Tip: Divide tuna mixture in 2 mason jars evenly. Place the remaining ingredients in the layers of, carrots, apples and spinach. Cover each jar with the lid tightly and refrigerate for about 1 day. Shake the jars well just before serving.

Nutritional Value:

- Calories 306
- Total Fat 1.8g
- Saturated Fat 0 g
- Cholesterol 63 mg
- Total Carbs 38 g
- Sugar 26 g
- Fiber 7.6 g
- Sodium 324 mg
- Potassium 602 mg
- Protein 35.8 g

Herring & Veggies Soup

Preparation Time: 15 minutes
Cooking Time: 25 minutes
Servings: 5

Ingredients:

- 2 tablespoons olive oil
- 1 shallot, chopped
- 2 small garlic cloves, minced
- 1 jalapeño pepper, chopped
- 1 head cabbage, chopped
- 1 small red bell pepper, seeded and chopped finely
- 1 small yellow bell pepper, seeded and chopped finely
- 5 cups low-sodium chicken broth
- 2 (4-ounce) boneless herring fillets, cubed
- ¼ cup fresh cilantro, minced
- 2 tablespoons fresh lemon juice
- Ground black pepper, as required
- 2 scallions, chopped

Method:

1. In a large soup pan, heat the oil over medium heat and sauté shallot and garlic for 2-3 minutes.
2. Add the cabbage and bell peppers and sauté for about 3-4 minutes.
3. Add the broth and bring to a boil over high heat.
4. Now, reduce the heat to medium-low and simmer for about 10 minutes.
5. Add the herring cubes and cook for about 5-6 minutes.
6. Stir in the cilantro, lemon juice, salt and black pepper and cook for about 1-2 minutes.
7. Serve hot with the topping of scallion.

Meal Prep Tip: Transfer the soup into a large bowl and set aside to cool. Divide the soup into 5 containers evenly. Cover the containers and refrigerate for 1-2 days. Reheat in the microwave before serving.

Nutritional Value:

- Calories 215
- Total Fat 11.2g
- Saturated Fat 2.1 g
- Cholesterol 35 mg
- Total Carbs 14.7 g
- Sugar 7 g
- Fiber 4.5 g
- Sodium 152 mg
- Potassium 574 mg
- Protein 15.1 g

Salmon Soup

Preparation Time: 15 minutes
Cooking Time: 20 minutes
Servings: 4

Ingredients:

- 1 tablespoon olive oil
- 1 yellow onion, chopped
- 1 garlic clove, minced
- 4 cups low-sodium chicken broth
- 1-pound boneless salmon, cubed
- 2 tablespoon fresh cilantro, chopped
- Ground black pepper, as required
- 1 tablespoon fresh lime juice

Method:

1. In a large pan heat the oil over medium heat and sauté the onion for about 5 minutes.
2. Add the garlic and sauté for about 1 minute.
3. Stir in the broth and bring to a boil over high heat.
4. Now, reduce the heat to low and simmer for about 10 minutes.
5. Add the salmon, and soy sauce and cook for about 3-4 minutes.
6. Stir in black pepper, lime juice, and cilantro and serve hot.

Meal Prep Tip: Transfer the soup into a large bowl and set aside to cool. Divide the soup into 4 containers evenly. Cover the containers and refrigerate for 1-2 days. Reheat in the microwave before serving.

Nutritional Value:

- Calories 208
- Total Fat 10.5 g
- Saturated Fat 1.5 g
- Cholesterol 50 mg
- Total Carbs 3.9 g
- Sugar 1.2 g
- Fiber 0.6 g
- Sodium 121 mg
- Potassium 331 mg
- Protein 24.4 g

Salmon & Shrimp Stew

Preparation Time: 20 minutes
Cooking Time: 21 minutes
Servings: 6

Ingredients:

- 2 tablespoons olive oil
- ½ cup onion, chopped finely
- 2 garlic cloves, minced
- 1 Serrano pepper, chopped
- 1 teaspoon smoked paprika
- 4 cups fresh tomatoes, chopped
- 4 cups low-sodium chicken broth
- 1-pound salmon fillets, cubed
- 1-pound shrimp, peeled and deveined
- 2 tablespoons fresh lime juice
- ¼ cup fresh basil, chopped
- ¼ cup fresh parsley, chopped
- Ground black pepper, as required
- 2 scallions, chopped

Method:

1. In a large soup pan, melt coconut oil over medium-high heat and sauté the onion for about 5-6 minutes.
2. Add the garlic, Serrano pepper and smoked paprika and sauté for about 1 minute.
3. Add the tomatoes and broth and bring to a gentle simmer over medium heat.
4. Simmer for about 5 minutes.
5. Add the salmon and simmer for about 3-4 minutes.
6. Stir in the remaining seafood and cook for about 4-5 minutes.
7. Stir in the lemon juice, basil, parsley, sea salt and black pepper and remove from heat.
8. Serve hot with the garnishing of scallion.

Meal Prep Tip: Transfer the stew into a large bowl and set aside to cool. Divide the stew into 4 containers evenly. Cover the containers and refrigerate for 1-2 days. Reheat in the microwave before serving.

Nutritional Value:

- Calories 271
- Total Fat 11 g
- Saturated Fat 1.8 g
- Cholesterol 193 mg
- Total Carbs 8.6 g
- Sugar 3.8 g
- Fiber 2.1 g
- Sodium 273 mg
- Potassium 763 mg
- Protein 34.7 g

Salmon Curry

Preparation Time: 15 minutes
Cooking Time: 30 minutes
Servings: 6

Ingredients:

- 6 (4-ounce) salmon fillets
- 1 teaspoon ground turmeric, divided
- Salt, as required
- 3 tablespoon olive oil, divided
- 1 yellow onion, chopped finely
- 1 teaspoon garlic paste
- 1 teaspoon fresh ginger paste
- 3-4 green chilies, halved
- 1 teaspoon red chili powder
- ½ teaspoon ground cumin
- ½ teaspoon ground cinnamon
- ¾ cup fat-free plain Greek yogurt, whipped
- ¾ cup filtered water
- 3 tablespoon fresh cilantro, chopped

Method:

1. Season each salmon fillet with ½ teaspoon of the turmeric and salt.
2. In a large skillet, melt 1 tablespoon of the butter over medium heat and cook the salmon fillets for about 2 minutes per side.
3. Transfer the salmon onto a plate.
4. In the same skillet, melt the remaining butter over medium heat and sauté the onion for about 4-5 minutes.
5. Add the garlic paste, ginger paste, green chilies, remaining turmeric and spices and sauté for about 1 minute.
6. Now, reduce the heat to medium-low.
7. Slowly, add the yogurt and water, stirring continuously until smooth.
8. Cover the skillet and simmer for about 10-15 minutes or until desired doneness of the sauce.
9. Carefully, add the salmon fillets and simmer for about 5 minutes.
10. Serve hot with the garnishing of cilantro.

Meal Prep Tip: Transfer the curry into a large bowl and set aside to cool. Divide the curry into 6 containers evenly. Cover the containers and refrigerate for 1-2 days. Reheat in the microwave before serving.

Nutritional Value:

- Calories 242
- Total Fat 14.3 g
- Saturated Fat 2 g
- Cholesterol 51 mg
- Total Carbs 4.1 g
- Sugar 2 g
- Fiber 0.8 g
- Sodium 98 mg
- Potassium 493 mg
- Protein 25.4 g

Salmon with Bell Peppers

Preparation Time: 15 minutes
Cooking Time: 20 minutes
Servings: 6

Ingredients:

- 6 (3-ounce) salmon fillets
- Pinch of salt
- Ground black pepper, as required
- 1 yellow bell pepper, seeded and cubed
- 1 red bell pepper, seeded and cubed
- 4 plum tomatoes, cubed
- 1 small onion, sliced thinly
- ½ cup fresh parsley, chopped
- ¼ cup olive oil
- 2 tablespoons fresh lemon juice

Method:

1. Preheat the oven to 400 degrees F.
2. Season each salmon fillet with salt and black pepper lightly.
3. In a bowl, mix together the bell peppers, tomato and onion.
4. Arrange 6 foil pieces onto a smooth surface.
5. Place 1 salmon fillet over each foil paper and sprinkle with salt and black pepper.
6. Place veggie mixture over each fillet evenly and top with parsley and capers evenly.
7. Drizzle with oil and lemon juice.
8. Fold each foil around salmon mixture to seal it.
9. Arrange the foil packets onto a large baking sheet in a single layer.
10. Bake for about 20 minutes.
11. Serve hot.

Meal Prep Tip: Transfer the salmon mixture into a large bowl and set aside to cool. Divide the salmon mixture into 6 containers evenly. Cover the containers and refrigerate for 1 day. Reheat in the microwave before serving.

Nutritional Value:

- Calories 220
- Total Fat 14 g
- Saturated Fat 2 g
- Cholesterol 38 mg
- Total Carbs 7.7 g
- Sugar 4.8 g
- Fiber 2 g
- Sodium 74 mg
- Potassium 647 mg
- Protein 17.9 g

Shrimp Salad

Preparation Time: 20 minutes
Cooking Time: 4 minutes
Servings: 6

Ingredients:

For Salad:

- 1-pound shrimp, peeled and deveined
- Salt and ground black pepper, as required
- 1 teaspoon olive oil
- 1½ cups carrots, peeled and julienned
- 1½ cups red cabbage, shredded
- 1½ cup cucumber, julienned
- 5 cups fresh baby arugula
- ¼ cup fresh basil, chopped
- ¼ cup fresh cilantro, chopped
- 4 cups lettuce, torn
- ¼ cup almonds, chopped

For Dressing:

- 2 tablespoons natural almond butter
- 1 garlic clove, crushed
- 1 tablespoon fresh cilantro, chopped
- 1 tablespoon fresh lime juice
- 1 tablespoon unsweetened applesauce
- 2 teaspoons balsamic vinegar
- ½ teaspoon cayenne pepper
- Salt, as required
- 1 tablespoon water
- 1/3 cup olive oil

Method:

1. Slowly, add the oil, beating continuously until smooth.
2. For salad: in a bowl, add shrimp, salt, black pepper and oil and toss to coat well.
3. Heat a skillet over medium-high heat and cook the shrimp for about 2 minutes per side.
4. Remove from the heat and set aside to cool.

5. In a large bowl, add the shrimp, vegetables and mix well.
6. For dressing: in a bowl, add all ingredients except oil and beat until well combined.
7. Place the dressing over shrimp mixture and gently, toss to coat well.
8. Serve immediately.

Meal Prep Tip: Divide dressing in 6 large mason jars evenly. Place the remaining ingredients in the layers of carrots, followed by cabbage, cucumber, arugula, basil, cilantro, shrimp, lettuce and almonds. Cover each jar with the lid tightly and refrigerate for about 1 day. Shake the jars well just before serving.

Nutritional Value:

- Calories 274
- Total Fat 17.7 g
- Saturated Fat 2.4 g
- Cholesterol 159 mg
- Total Carbs 10 g
- Sugar 3.8 g
- Fiber 2.9 g
- Sodium 242 mg
- Potassium 481 mg
- Protein 20.5 g

Shrimp & Veggies Curry

Preparation Time: 20 minutes
Cooking Time: 20 minutes
Servings: 6

Ingredients:

- 2 teaspoons olive oil
- 1½ medium white onions, sliced
- 2 medium green bell peppers, seeded and sliced
- 3 medium carrots, peeled and sliced thinly
- 3 garlic cloves, chopped finely
- 1 tablespoon fresh ginger, chopped finely
- 2½ teaspoons curry powder
- 1½ pounds shrimp, peeled and deveined
- 1 cup filtered water
- 2 tablespoons fresh lime juice
- Salt and ground black pepper, as required
- 2 tablespoons fresh cilantro, chopped

Method:

1. In a large skillet, heat oil over medium-high heat and sauté the onion for about 4-5 minutes.
2. Add the bell peppers and carrot and sauté for about 3-4 minutes.
3. Add the garlic, ginger and curry powder and sauté for about 1 minute.
4. Add the shrimp and sauté for about 1 minute.
5. Stir in the water and cook for about 4-6 minutes, stirring occasionally.
6. Stir in lime juice and remove from heat.
7. Serve hot with the garnishing of cilantro.

Meal Prep Tip: Transfer the curry into a large bowl and set aside to cool. Divide the curry into 6 containers evenly. Cover the containers and refrigerate for 1-2 days. Reheat in the microwave before serving.

Nutritional Value:

- Calories 193
- Total Fat 3.8 g
- Saturated Fat 0.9 g
- Cholesterol 239 mg
- Total Carbs 12 g
- Sugar 4.7 g
- Fiber 2.3 g
- Sodium 328 mg
- Potassium 437 mg
- Protein 27.1 g

Shrimp with Zucchini

Preparation Time: 20 minutes
Cooking Time: 8 minutes
Servings: 4

Ingredients:

- 3 tablespoons olive oil
- 1-pound medium shrimp, peeled and deveined
- 1 shallot, minced
- 4 garlic cloves, minced
- ¼ teaspoon red pepper flakes, crushed
- Salt and ground black pepper, as required
- ¼ cup low-sodium chicken broth
- 2 tablespoons fresh lemon juice
- 1 teaspoon fresh lemon zest, grated finely
- ½ pound zucchini, spiralized with Blade C

Method:

1. In a large skillet, heat the oil and butter over medium-high heat and cook the shrimp, shallot, garlic, red pepper flakes, salt and black pepper for about 2 minutes, stirring occasionally.
2. Stir in the broth, lemon juice and lemon zest and bring to a gentle boil.
3. Stir in zucchini noodles and cook for about 1-2 minutes.
4. Serve hot.

Meal Prep Tip: Transfer the shrimp mixture into a large bowl and set aside to cool. Divide the shrimp mixture into 4 containers. Cover the containers and refrigerate for about 1-2 days. Reheat in microwave before serving.

Nutritional Value:

- Calories 245
- Total Fat 12.6 g
- Saturated Fat 2.2 g
- Cholesterol 239 mg
- Total Carbs 5.8 g
- Sugar 1.2 g
- Fiber 08 g
- Sodium 289 mg
- Potassium 381 mg
- Protein 27 g

Shrimp with Broccoli

Preparation Time: 15 minutes
Cooking Time: 12 minutes
Servings: 6

Ingredients:

- 2 tablespoons olive oil, divided
- 4 cups broccoli, chopped
- 2-3 tablespoons filtered water
- 1½ pounds large shrimp, peeled and deveined
- 2 garlic cloves, minced
- 1 (1-inch) piece fresh ginger, minced
- Salt and ground black pepper, as required

Method:

1. In a large skillet, heat 1 tablespoon of oil over medium-high heat and cook the broccoli for about 1-2 minutes stirring continuously.
2. Stir in the water and cook, covered for about 3-4 minutes, stirring occasionally.
3. With a spoon, push the broccoli to side of the pan.
4. Add the remaining oil and let it heat.
5. Add the shrimp and cook for about 1-2 minutes, tossing occasionally.
6. Add the remaining ingredients and sauté for about 2-3 minutes.
7. Serve hot.

Meal Prep Tip: Transfer the shrimp mixture into a large bowl and set aside to cool. Divide the shrimp mixture into 6 containers evenly. Cover the containers and refrigerate for 1 day. Reheat in the microwave before serving.

Nutritional Value:

- Calories 197
- Total Fat 6.8 g
- Saturated Fat 1.3 g
- Cholesterol 239 mg
- Total Carbs 6.1 g
- Sugar 1.1 g
- Fiber 1.6 g
- Sodium 324 mg
- Potassium 389 mg
- Protein 27.6 g

Chapter 9: Dessert Recipes

Frozen Vanilla Yogurt

Preparation Time: 10 minutes
Servings: 6

Ingredients:

- 3 cups fat-free plain Greek yogurt
- 4-6 drops liquid stevia
- 1 teaspoon organic vanilla extract
- ¼ cup fresh strawberries, hulled and sliced

Method:

1. In a bowl, add all the ingredients except strawberries and mix until well combined.
2. Transfer the mixture into an ice cream maker and process according to manufacturer's directions.
3. Transfer the mixture into a bowl and freeze, covered for about 30-40 minutes or until desired consistency.
4. Garnish with strawberry slices and serve.

Meal Prep Tip: Line a cookie sheet with parchment paper. With a cookie scooper, place the yogurt portion onto the prepared cookie sheet. Freeze overnight. Remove from the freezer and transfer the frozen yogurt balls into an airtight container. Store in freezer up to 1 week. Remove from the freezer and set aside for 15-20 minutes before serving.

Nutritional Value:

- Calories 74
- Total Fat 0.3 g
- Saturated Fat 0 g
- Cholesterol 4mg
- Total Carbs 5.6 g
- Sugar 4.9 g
- Fiber 0.1 g
- Sodium 58 mg
- Potassium 10 mg
- Protein 12 g

Spinach Sorbet

Preparation Time: 15 minutes
Servings: 4

Ingredients:

- 3 cups fresh spinach, chopped
- 1 tablespoon fresh basil leaves
- ½ of avocado, peeled, pitted and chopped
- ¾ cup unsweetened almond milk
- 20 drops liquid stevia
- 1 teaspoon almonds, chopped very finely
- 1 teaspoon organic vanilla extract
- 1 cup ice cubes

Method:

1. In a blender, add all ingredients and pulse until creamy and smooth.
2. Transfer into an ice cream maker and process according to manufacturer's directions.
3. Transfer into an airtight container and freeze for at least 4-5 hours before serving.

Meal Prep Tip: Transfer the sorbet into a shallow, flat container. With a plastic wrap, cover the ice cream and store in the back of the freezer.

Nutritional Value:

- Calories 70
- Total Fat 5.9 g
- Saturated Fat 1.1 g
- Cholesterol 0 mg
- Total Carbs 3.6 g
- Sugar 0.4 g
- Fiber 2.4 g
- Sodium 53 mg
- Potassium 290 mg
- Protein 1.4 g

Avocado Mousse

Preparation Time: 15 minutes
Servings: 3

Ingredients:

- 2 ripe Haas avocados, peeled, pitted and chopped roughly
- 1 teaspoon liquid stevia
- 1 teaspoon organic vanilla extract
- Pinch of salt

Method:

1. In a high-speed blender, add all the ingredients and pulse until smooth.
2. Transfer the pudding into a serving bowl.
3. Cover the bowl and refrigerate to chill for at least 2 hours before serving.

Meal Prep Tip: Transfer the mousse into an airtight container. Cover the containers and refrigerate for about 1 day.

Nutritional Value:

- Calories 277
- Total Fat 26.1 g
- Saturated Fat 5.5 g
- Cholesterol 0 mg
- Total Carbs 11.7 g
- Sugar 0.9 g
- Fiber 8 g
- Sodium 59 mg
- Potassium 652 mg
- Protein 2.6g

Strawberry Mousse

Preparation Time: 15 minutes
Servings: 6

Ingredients:

- 1½ cups fresh strawberries, hulled
- 1 2/3 cups chilled unsweetened almond milk
- 2-3 drops liquid stevia
- 1 teaspoon organic vanilla extract

Method:

1. In a food processor, add all the ingredients and pulse until smooth.
2. Transfer into serving bowls and serve.

Meal Prep Tip: Transfer the mousse into an airtight container. Cover the containers and refrigerate for up to 3 days.

Nutritional Value:

- Calories 25
- Total Fat 1.1g
- Saturated Fat 0.1 g
- Cholesterol 0 mg
- Total Carbs 3.4 g
- Sugar 1.9 g
- Fiber 1 g
- Sodium 50 mg
- Potassium 109 mg
- Protein 0.5 g

Blueberries Pudding

Preparation Time: 10 minutes
Servings: 3

Ingredients:

- 1 small avocado, peeled, pitted and chopped
- 1 cup frozen blueberries
- ¼ teaspoon fresh ginger, grated freshly
- 1 teaspoon lime zest, grated finely
- 2 tablespoons fresh lime juice
- 10 drops liquid stevia
- 5 tablespoons filtered water

Method:

1. In a blender, add all the ingredients and pulse till creamy and smooth.
2. Transfer into serving bowls and serve.

Meal Prep Tip: Transfer the pudding into an airtight container. Cover the containers and refrigerate for up to 2 days.

Nutritional Value:

- Calories 166
- Total Fat 13.3 g
- Saturated Fat 4.2.8 g
- Cholesterol 0 mg
- Total Carbs 13.1 g
- Sugar 5.2 g
- Fiber 5.8 g
- Sodium 4 mg
- Potassium 331 mg
- Protein 1.7 g

Raspberry Chia Pudding

Preparation Time: 10 minutes
Servings: 4

Ingredients:

- 1½ cups unsweetened almond milk
- 1¼ cups fresh raspberries
- ½ cup chia seeds
- 1 tablespoon flax meal
- 3-4 drops liquid stevia
- 2 teaspoons organic vanilla extract

Method:

1. In a blender, add the almond milk and raspberries and pulse until smooth.
2. Transfer the milk mixture into a large bowl.
3. Add the remaining ingredients except raspberries and stir until well combined.
4. Refrigerate to chill for at least 1 hour before serving.

Meal Prep Tip: Transfer the pudding into an airtight container. Cover the containers and refrigerate for about 1 day.

Nutritional Value:

- Calories 107
- Total Fat 7.2 g
- Saturated Fat 0.5 g
- Cholesterol 0 mg
- Total Carbs 12.1 g
- Sugar 2 g
- Fiber 8.4 g
- Sodium 68 mg
- Potassium 246 mg
- Protein 4.2 g

Brown Rice Pudding

Preparation Time: 15 minutes
Cooking Time: 30 minutes
Servings: 4

Ingredients:

- 2 cups low-fat milk
- 1/3 cup Erythritol
- 1½ teaspoons organic vanilla extract
- ¼ teaspoon ground cinnamon
- 1 egg
- 2 cups cooked brown rice

Method:

1. In a medium pan, add the milk, Erythritol, vanilla extract and cinnamon over medium-high heat and bring to a boil, stirring continuously.
2. Remove from the heat.
3. In a large bowl, add the egg and beat well.
4. Slowly, add the hot milk mixture, a little bit at a time and beat until well combined.
5. In the same pan, add the milk mixture and rice and
6. Place the 2 cups of cooked rice into the pan used to cook the milk mixture and stir to combine.
7. Place the pan over medium-high heat and bring to a boil, stirring continuously.
8. Reduce heat to low and simmer for about 15-20 minutes, stirring after every 5 minutes.
9. Remove from the heat and transfer into a bowl.
10. With a wax paper, cover the top of pudding and refrigerate to chill before serving.

Meal Prep Tip: Transfer the pudding into an airtight container. Cover the containers and refrigerate for up to 2 days.

Nutritional Value:

- Calories 416
- Total Fat 4.8 g
- Saturated Fat 1.6 g
- Cholesterol 47 mg
- Total Carbs 78 g
- Sugar 6 g
- Fiber 3.3 g
- Sodium 73 mg
- Potassium 455 mg
- Protein 12.5 g

Lemon Cookies

Preparation Time: 10 minutes
Cooking Time: 12 minutes
Servings: 6

Ingredients:

- ¼ cup unsweetened applesauce
- 1 cup cashew butter
- 1 teaspoon fresh lemon zest, grated finely
- 2 tablespoons fresh lemon juice
- Pinch of sea salt

Method:

1. Preheat the oven to 350 degrees F. Line a large cookie sheet with parchment paper.
2. In a food processor, add all ingredients and pulse until smooth.
3. With a tablespoon, place the mixture onto prepared cookie sheet in a single layer.
4. Bake for about 12 minutes or until golden brown.
5. Remove from oven and place the cookie sheet onto a wire rack to cool for about 5 minutes.
6. Carefully invert the cookies onto wire rack to cool completely before serving.

Meal Prep Tip: Store these cookies in an airtight container, by placing parchment papers between the cookies to avoid the sticking. These cookies can be stored in the refrigerator for up to 2 weeks.

Nutritional Value:

- Calories 257
- Total Fat 21.9 g
- Saturated Fat 4.2 g
- Cholesterol 0 mg
- Total Carbs 13.1 g
- Sugar 1.2 g
- Fiber 1 g
- Sodium 47 mg
- Potassium 248 mg
- Protein 7.6 g

Yogurt Cheesecake

Preparation Time: 15 minutes
Cooking Time: 35 minutes
Servings: 8

Ingredients:

- 2½ cups fat-free plain Greek yogurt
- 6-8 drops liquid stevia
- 3 egg whites
- 1/3 cup cacao powder
- ¼ cup arrowroot starch
- 1 teaspoon organic vanilla extract
- Pinch of sea salt

Method:

1. Preheat the oven to 35 degrees F. Grease a 9-inch cake pan.
2. In a large bowl, add all ingredients and mix until well combined.
3. Place the mixture into the prepared pan evenly.
4. Bake for about 30-35 minutes.
5. Remove from oven and let it cool completely.
6. Refrigerate to chill for about 3-4 hours or until set completely.
7. Cut into 8 equal sized slices and serve.

Meal Prep Tip: With foil pieces, wrap the cheesecake slices and refrigerate for about 1-3 days. Reheat in the microwave before serving.

Nutritional Value:

- Calories 74
- Total Fat 0.9g
- Saturated Fat 0.4 g
- Cholesterol 2 mg
- Total Carbs 8.5 g
- Sugar 3 g
- Fiber 1.1 g
- Sodium 89 mg
- Potassium 21 mg
- Protein 9.5 g

Conclusion

The major aim of this cookbook was to provide an idea of managing a diabetic diet while putting the meal prep up to the best use. Life is tough and cooking every other day makes it harder to manage time; meal prepping in this regard brings convenience. This cookbook, therefore, shares good food and delicious recipes for all diabetic patients or those who want to prevent the ills of this disorder. The extensive range of recipes along with meal prep tips gives a wholesome package to all the readers. Divided into different segments; all the shared recipes can meet the daily needs of an individual as well a whole family.

www.ingramcontent.com/pod-product-compliance
Lightning Source LLC
Chambersburg PA
CBHW081402070526
44583CB00020B/2647